Chester Himes

Twayne's United States Authors Series

Warren French, Editor

University of Wales, Swansea

TUSAS 553

CHESTER HIMES
Courtesy of the Yale Collection of American Literature,
Beinecke Rare Book and Manuscript Library,
Yale University.

Chester Himes

By Gilbert H. Muller

LaGuardia Community College
The City University of New York

Twayne Publishers
A Division of G. K. Hall & Co. • *Boston*

Chester Himes
Gilbert H. Muller

Copyright 1989 by G. K. Hall & Co.
All rights reserved.
Published by Twayne Publishers
A Division of G. K. Hall & Co.
70 Lincoln Street
Boston, Massachusetts 02111

Copyediting supervised by Barbara Sutton
Book production by Gabrielle B. McDonald
Book design by Barbara Anderson

Typeset in 11 pt. Garamond
by Compositors Corporation, Cedar Rapids, Iowa

Printed on permanent/durable acid-free paper
and bound in the United States of America

Library of Congress Cataloging-in-Publication Data

Muller, Gilbert H., 1941–
       Chester Himes / by Gilbert H. Muller.
              p.   cm. — (Twayne's United States author series; TUSAS 553)
       Bibliography: p.
       Includes index.
       ISBN 0-8057-7545-5 (alk. paper)
       1. Himes, Chester B., 1909–   —Criticism and interpretation.
I. Title.   II. Series.
PS3515.I713Z78   1989
813'.54—dc20   89–32310
                                                                              CIP

For
Laleh, Parisa and Darius

Contents

About the Author

Gilbert H. Muller received his B.A. from the University of Kentucky in 1963, his M.A. from Stanford University in 1966, and his Ph.D. in English and American literature from Stanford in 1967. Currently professor of English at the LaGuardia campus of the City University of New York, he has also taught at Shiraz University and Damavand College in Iran, at Stanford University, and at Vassar College.

Muller is the author of *Nightmares and Visions: Flannery O'Connor and the Catholic Grotesque* (1972), which won the Parks Award for the best study of southern fiction and was listed as one of the outstanding works in criticism in 1973 by the Association of College and Research Libraries. He has also published *John A. Williams* in the Twayne Authors Series. His essays and reviews have appeared in such publications as the *New York Times,* the *New Republic,* the *Nation,* the *New Leader, Newsday,* the *Sewanee Review,* the *Georgia Review, Studies in Short Fiction,* and *Renascence.* He is a noted author of textbooks in English and composition, including *The American College Handbook, The McGraw-Hill Introduction to Literature, The Short Prose Reader,* and *The McGraw-Hill Reader.* He has received grants from the National Endowment for the Humanities, the Mellon Foundation, the Fulbright Commission, and other programs.

Preface

Ralph Ellison has observed that American readers reject serious fiction until its time has passed and it has lost its moral cutting edge. The fiction of Chester Himes—indeed the entire life and career of the artist—is a case in point. Himes's career started auspiciously enough when the young convict's stories began appearing in 1934 in issues of *Esquire* that also included the work of Hemingway, Fitzgerald, and Dos Passos. Yet America largely ignored Himes for the next forty years, even as he was establishing a loyal popular and critical audience in Europe. In 1952 Paris reviewers selected his *Lonely Crusade* as one of the five best books by an American author that had been published in France during the past decade, and more European awards followed. But in the United States, Himes remained unknown. Aside from a flurry of interest in him in the late 1970s, caused in large part by the success of the film adaptation of his *Cotton Comes to Harlem,* Chester Bomar Himes has been a forgotten figure in contemporary American literature.

Himes has one of the most radical, unforgiving, and coldly absurdist visions of the American experience in contemporary literature—a fact that contributes to his critical neglect. His novels provide, as H. Bruce Franklin observes in the best essay on Himes (in *The Victim as Criminal and Artist*), "a miniature social history of the United States from World War II through the days of the Black urban rebellions of the 1960s." Much of this "social history" was conditioned by Himes's experiences as an inmate at the Ohio State Penitentiary from 1929 to 1936. Himes was nineteen when he went to prison for armed robbery and twenty-six when he was released. His social vision centered at first on the psychological consequences of violence and racism and then increasingly on absurdity and apocalypse. Following controversy over his first two novels, *If He Hollers Let Him Go* (1945) and *Lonely Crusade* (1947), and dismissal of his superlative prison novel, *Cast the First Stone* (1952), as hopelessly neurotic, Himes sailed for Europe. He remained in relatively permanent exile in Paris, Spain, and elsewhere. Ailing and incontinent by 1970, his career was behind him—except for the two-volume autobiography he completed during this period.

Himes died on the coast of Spain in 1984. His exile was self-imposed but caused also by the failure of the American literary establishment to come to terms with his radical, progressively grotesque cultural vision. That an author who wrote seventeen novels, dozens of collected and uncollected stories and essays, and a significant two-volume autobiography should be largely unknown offers a chilling prognosis for the state of our literary culture today.

Several features make Himes a significant American writer. *If He Hollers Let Him Go* and *Lonely Crusade* offer one of the most vivid and coherent pictures of World War II Los Angeles culture in American fiction and mark a watershed in the tradition of proletarian fiction. *Cast the First Stone* is an important contribution to the special genre of prison fiction. Himes's impressive cycle of detective novels set in Harlem constitutes a unique antigenre in crime fiction. His notable autobiography offers an intellectual history of the African-American writer in exile, as well as evidence of Himes's relationship to the European traditions of existentialism and the absurd. Himes's work overall reveals a persistent effort to explore unpleasant truths and basic absurdities in American culture.

Beneath Himes's critique of American society is a progressive impulse literally to reject culture, to embrace an anarchistic and absurdist vision of a world without meaning. This study of Himes offers a coherent assessment of the author's evolving vision of contemporary absurdity, beginning with the early novels in which characters attempt to affirm middle-class values and lives and ending in urban apocalypse as Himes's Harlem cycle (nine novels, 1957–69) comes to a close with *Blind Man with a Pistol* and "Plan B." There is a concomitant evaluation of the literary modes Himes developed to express his evolving vision. His style in his early years was serviceable but, as James Baldwin acknowledged in an early review of *If He Hollers Let Him Go,* "uneven and awkward." Nevertheless, when Himes moved away from a naturalistic style toward the taut one first used in *Cast the First Stone,* he opened a new field of vision for himself. He found his best stylistic options in the tradition of detective fiction, which he had started to read during his prison years. This was the style—spare, violent, explosive, urban—that would lead him toward existentialist and absurdist possibilities in fiction.

To view the world of Chester Himes in the context of conflicting and progressively disintegrating patterns of bourgeois culture is to understand the man, appreciate the evolution of his radically grotesque vision, and perceive his significance as a writer. Hime's first five novels, highly autobiographical and heavily influenced by the traditions of psychological realism and proletarian naturalism, reveal protagonists with ambivalent attitudes toward middle-class culture. These protagonists are men of intellect who discover that they are doomed by history and culture. If there is a dominant theme in *If He Hollers Let Him Go, Lonely Crusade, Cast the First Stone, The Third Generation,* and *The Primitive,* it is the stark paralysis of personality and culture.

In his detective fiction, Himes distances himself from confessional materials, creating a universe where paralysis of personality is still apparent (Grave Digger and Coffin Ed, Himes's two black detectives, ultimately are unable to solve crimes) but where the world itself runs out of control. At the end of *Blind Man with a Pistol,* Himes's two detectives, the antiheroes of his antigenre, take potshots at rats fleeing a burning tenement while a race riot engulfs the Harlem community. This penchant for the absurd enables Himes to explore a dehumanized culture that is increasingly grotesque and incapable of redemption. The situations that Himes places his protagonists in become more outrageous and absurd, trapping them in the prison house of culture.

Himes demonstrates more vividly and persistently than most other contemporary writers the absurdities of both racism and capitalist culture. If he has been attacked by certain critics as being a racist himself, Himes would have responded that he tried to write the truth as he saw it. The larger truth is that Himes should be rescued from critical obscurity, for his perception of the truths inherent in the grotesqueries of American culture constitutes an original literary vision.

Gilbert H. Muller

LaGuardia Community College
The City University of New York

Acknowledgments

I would like to thank John A. Williams for his invaluable assistance in developing this study. His material on Himes—notably letters and a copy of the manuscript of "Plan B"—were helpful in developing a coherent assessment of Himes's career. I also appreciate the permission extended by the Beinecke Library at Yale University and the University of Rochester Library to quote from their manuscript holdings. Finally, I am pleased once again to acknowledge the warmth and support of Warren French in sponsoring this study of Chester Himes.

Chronology

1909   Chester Himes born 29 July in Jefferson City, Missouri, to Joseph Sandy Himes and Estelle Bomar Himes, the youngest of three children. Father teaches at Lincoln Institute.

1914–1920   Moves with family to Cleveland, Ohio, then to Lorman, Mississippi, where father becomes chairman of the Mechanical Arts Department, Alcorn College.

1921–1923   Lives with mother and brother Joseph in Augusta, Georgia, where he attends Haines Institute and Mrs. Himes teaches. Entire family then moves to Pine Bluff, Arkansas. Father teaches at Branch Normal Institute. Brother Joseph loses eyesight in school accident, and family moves to Saint Louis where he can be treated.

1925   Family returns to Cleveland.

1926   Graduates in January from Cleveland's Glenville High School. Working as busboy at Wade Park Manor Hotel, falls down elevator shaft and is seriously injured.

1926–1928   Enters Ohio State University on disability income. Leaves in 1927 because of poor health and failing grades. In Cleveland, works as bellhop at Gilsey Hotel, gravitating to city's criminal underworld.

1928   Arrested twice for armed robbery, convicted and sentenced on 27 December to from twenty to twenty-five years in Ohio State Penitentiary.

1929–1936   Spends seven and a half years in Ohio State Prison in Columbus—five years in main prison where famous fire of 1930 occurred and two and a half years on prison farm.

1932–1936   First crime fiction published in the *Pittsburgh Courier, Bronzeman, Atlanta Daily World, Abbott's Monthly Magazine,* and *Esquire.*

1936   Paroled from prison in May; returns to Cleveland.

1937   Marries Jean Lucinda Johnson, 13 August. Writes first version of prison novel, *Black Sheep* (retitled *Cast the First Stone*).

1937–1938   Employed by Works Progress Administration as laborer. Promoted to research assistant for Cleveland Public Library. Assigned to Ohio Writer's Project to write official history of Cleveland.

1939   Writes unsigned column, "This Cleveland," for *Cleveland Daily News*. Works on author Louis Bromfield's Malabar Farm as butler.

1940–1944   Moves with wife to Los Angeles. Works in war industry in Los Angeles and San Francisco. Writes stories and essays for *Crisis* and *Opportunity*.

1944   Awarded Rosenwald Fellowship to finish novel, *If He Hollers Let Him Go*. Moves to New York City.

1945   *If He Hollers Let Him Go*. Returns to northern California, living in rural Susanville and working on second novel.

1946   Returns to New York City.

1947   *Lonely Crusade*.

1948   Spends May and June at Yaddo Writer's Colony, Saratoga Springs, New York.

1950   Separates from wife.

1952   *Cast the First Stone*.

1953   Leaves United States for Paris.

1954   *The Third Generation*. Moves to Mallorca.

1955   *The Primitive*.

1956   In Paris, begins writing detective fiction for Gallimard's "La Série noire" at suggestion of Marcel Duhamel.

1957   *For Love of Imabelle*. Spends part of year in Denmark.

1958   French translation of *For Love of Imabelle* wins Grand prix for year's best detective novel.

1959   *The Crazy Kill* and *The Real Cool Killers*. Begins relationship with Lesley Packard.

1960   *All Shot Up* and *The Big Gold Dream*.

1961   *Pinktoes*.

1962   Travels to United States for *France-Soir* to do film documentary on Harlem.

1963   *Une Affair de viol (A case of rape)*. Suffers stroke in Sisal, Mexico. Returns to France.

1965   *Cotton Comes to Harlem*. Marries Lesley Packard.

1965–1966   Resides in La Ciotat in southern France. Travels to Paris, London, Barcelona, Sweden, Egypt.

1966   *Run Man Run* and *The Heat's On*.

1968–1969   Moves to Alicante, Spain, with Packard. Builds house in Moraira.

1969   *Blind Man with a Pistol*.

1970   Film version of *Cotton Comes to Harlem*.

1972   *The Quality of Hurt*. Travels to New York; recognized for achievements on 12 March at Carnegie Endowment for International Peace.

1973   *Black on Black*.

1974   Film version of *The Heat's On*, retitled *Come Back Charleston Blue*.

1976   *My Life of Absurdity*.

1983   *Plan B* published in French by Lieu Commun.

1984   Dies 12 November in Moraira, Spain.

1985   *A Case of Rape* published in United States.

Chapter One

Chester Himes: His Life of Absurdity

Born into a middle-class African-American family in Jefferson City, Missouri, on 29 July 1909, Chester Bomar Himes grew to adulthood and old age with an intensifying conviction that his life served as testament to the grotesque forces of contemporary Western civilization. As a young writer, he published his first fiction while in prison, serving a twenty- to twenty-five-year sentence for armed robbery. He had entered Ohio State Penitentiary in 1928 at the age of nineteen and was released seven years later. Undervalued as a writer in the United States in the 1930s and 1940s, he went into exile in 1953, discovering belatedly a measure of literary fame, first in France and then internationally. Today his reputation rests not so much on an important body of earlier confessional fiction as on his *policiers noires*, a cycle of nine detective novels presenting a panorama of Harlem as the center of absurdity for black Americans in the modern world. Given the ludicrous and harrowing vagaries of his long life and the striking grotesquerie of his fiction, it was fitting that Chester Himes titled the last book he would write, the second volume of his autobiography, *My Life of Absurdity.*

Whereas Richard Chase in *The American Novel and Its Tradition* extols the "great practical sanity" of the English novel, we must acknowledge the great *in*sanity in practice of much American fiction, notably the fiction of Chester Himes. If literature reflects culture, if it can serve as a way to carbon-date the American heritage, then we must contend with those trace elements of absurdity that coalesce in writers as diverse as Melville, Twain, Faulkner, Flannery O'Connor, Ellison, and Chester Himes. The absurd in American literature is an attempt to subvert the evils of society. It speaks comically and demonically to the defects in culture. As Himes put it in a one-paragraph preface to his last superlative detective novel, *Blind Man with a Pistol* (1969):

A friend of mine, Phil Lomax, told me this story about a blind man with a pistol shooting at a man who had slapped him on a subway train and killing an innocent bystander peacefully reading his newspaper across the aisle and I thought, damn

right, sounds like today's news, riots in the ghettoes, war in Vietnam, masochistic do-
ings in the Middle East. And then I thought of some of our loudmouthed leaders
urging our more vulnerable soul brothers on to getting themselves killed, and
thought further that all unorganized violence is like a blind man with a pistol.[1]

For Himes, absurdity is in the American grain. It arises from the gulf between
American pretensions and realities, from the "irreconcilability of American
ideals and American experience," as one astute English commentator asserts.[2]
From the beginning of his literary career in 1931 to the end, Chester Himes
used the absurd element in his fiction as a political weapon—as a rhetoric of
protest against the blindness of American society as a whole.

The Autobiography

Himes's vision of absurdity was molded by the outlines of his life. In fact,
his two-volume autobiography—*The Quality of Hurt* (1972) and *My Life of
Absurdity* (1976)—can be read concurrently as personal, artistic, and cultural definitions, at once serious and comic, of Himes's transcontinental and
intercontinental passage across a grotesque contemporary landscape. From
Jefferson City to the seaside village of Moraira, Spain, where he lived for the
last fifteen years of his life, the obtrusive force of the grotesque was not lost on
the artist and the man. Rephrasing D. H. Lawrence's assessment of earlier
American writers, with Chester Himes we must be prepared to trust both the
artist and his absurd tale.

The autobiography of Chester Himes provides the indispensable clue to
the man and the artist. Himes represses nothing—not his disdain for many
people and their cultures, his chauvinistic and sexist behavior, his encompass-
ing anger and hurt over America's working of his fate. Yet throughout the
two volumes of his autobiography is also an ironic and corrosive deflation of
culture's ability to kill him off. As he declares on the dust jacket of *The Quality of Hurt*, "When America kills a nigger it expects him to remain dead. . . .
But I didn't know I was supposed to die. I still had hope I still believed in the
devil." To embrace the demonic is Chester Himes's method of subduing the
grotesque elements of his existence.[3] Through autobiographical memory,
Himes recounts the dreadful fate created for him and also his refusal to succumb to it.

Himes begins the first volume of his autobiography on a note of droll absurdity: he cannot remember why he came to Europe, what his prison experiences had been like, or how the exact contours of "America's sex and racism
syndrome" shaped his life.[4] From this brisk ironic apologia, the author thus

resolves, however awkwardly, to encompass himself, Chester Himes, not a skeleton or invisible man, not yet posthumous, but rather ruthlessly insistent on discovering the shape and sources of his identity. Was his fate absurd and puppetlike, purely determined? Or could he, as Himes intimates, fight back through writing?

The youngest of three sons, Chester Himes was the product of what he terms in *The Quality of Hurt* as racial and genetic "opposites"—a mother who was light-skinned, "octoroon," and aristocratic, whose family also had Native American lineage; and a father who was "a short black man with bowed legs, a perfect elipsoidal skull, and an Arabic face with a big hooked nose" (5). His father, Professor Joseph Sandy Himes, taught blacksmithing and wheelwrighting as the head of the Mechanical Department at Lincoln Institute, now Lincoln University. His mother, descended from the Bomars of English nobility, pressured Himes with the ambiguous injunction to live up to his "heritage." Himes describes his features in terms touched by this amalgam of grotesque opposites: "My hair is kinky, my complexion sepia, my features might be handsome were my nose not so tiny, and my skull's so flat and misshapen the students of my father used to say he had made it in a blacksmith shop" (5). Early in the autobiography, we grow accustomed to the interlacing of opposites, discontinuities, distortions, and deformities that create an absurd or irrational motif in Himes's life.

Between 1913 and 1926, when the author entered Ohio State University, the Himes family was constantly moving, the passage itself a product of growing contemporary social complexities. Although they had education, class, and caste for cachet, the family by virtue of their race was still excommunicated by white culture. In 1917 Professor Himes lost his job at Alcorn A&M in Mississippi, largely because he was the only black man in the county to own a car, a Studebaker. By 1922 he was working as a waiter in a St. Louis beer hall, a city the family had moved to in order to have their son Joe's blindness treated properly. Earlier that year, Joe, who would attend Oberlin and Ohio State and ultimately become a professor of sociology, had been injured when his chemistry experiment exploded during a school demonstration.

In 1923 Joseph Himes moved the family to Cleveland, Ohio, where they lived with his relatives, whom Mrs. Himes could not abide. Eventually Professor Himes found work as a carpenter and bought a house in the white neighborhood of Glenville. Chester graduated from Glenville High School in January 1926. Although he had received a 56 on his Latin examination, it had been transformed to an 86 through a clerical error, and he was eligible for admission to Ohio State.

University Days

Although Chester Himes had always felt marginally alienated from the schools he had attended, he enrolled nevertheless at Ohio State University in September 1926. He arrived with a latent trust of society yet looking as if he was the product of a cosmic cataclysm. He registered at Ohio State literally black and blue, braced and trussed as a result of a near-fatal accident while working as a busboy at the Wade Park Manor Hotel in 1926. He had fallen down the shaft of an open elevator, seriously maiming himself: "My chin had hit something that cut the flesh to the bone, broke my lower jaw, and shattered all my teeth. My left arm hit something and both bones broke just above the wrist so that they came out through the skin, dead white with drops of blood in the bone fractures. My spine hit something and the last three vertebrae were fractured"(20). Turned away from a white hospital, he was operated on at Huron Road Hospital. He began therapy and was placed on a $75 monthly disability pension by the Ohio State Industrial Commission. With a back brace, dental work, and a monthly stipend, Himes entered Ohio State, where he scored the fourth highest IQ on the standardized entrance examinations.

Prior to his enrollment at Ohio State, Himes had had a relatively benign impression of American society. He once confessed to friend and fellow author John A. Williams: "I was a good boy. I saved my money, took care of my health, and entered Ohio State University that fall. Somehow, even in the south, up until then I had been sheltered from the impact of race prejudice. Looking back, I wonder how it was possible, but I had always felt superior to the southern crackers and rednecks whom I had seen. Ohio State University changed that."[5] Columbus and Ohio State, a city and an academic institution rigorously Jim-Crowed, would thwart this bright young student's dreams.

"What if history were a madman?" asks Ellison's Invisible Man. When Himes positions his own life against any moment in history, he seems to be a voyager in a wonderful, horrifying, potentially ludicrous realm. Roger Rosenblatt alludes to this "sense of circus or madhouse that controls much black autobiography," and it is a circus that Himes entered at Ohio State.[6] "I bought a coonskin coat for three hundred dollars," Himes writes in *The Quality of Hurt*, "a Knickerbocker suit, a long-stemmed pipe, and a Model T Ford roadster, and I became a collegian"(25). His wishful thinking clashes with the Jim-Crow realities of segregated university life, a duality of which Himes rapidly became conscious. Ultimately he was nauseated by his masquerading in a white environment.

If Himes's role playing as a collegian involved self-deception, his gradual movement into a criminal life was an attempt to investigate reality from another perspective. Withdrawing from Ohio State in the spring of 1927 for reasons of "ill health and failing grades," Himes returned to Cleveland, sick and psychologically exhausted, largely unprepared for the persistent quarreling of his parents that would end a year later with Joseph Himes's leaving for good. By the summer, Himes was immersed in the gambling world of Cleveland's black ghetto. He was an associate of "Bunch Boy," who ran a gambling club, and other characters whom Himes would reconstitute much later in fiction: "Some of the regulars were Abie the Jew, Red Johnny, Four-Four, Chink Charlie, Dummy, and other characters I've used in my detective story series" (36).

Ohio State and the Cleveland ghetto were dual constituents in Himes's early education or quest for self. In autobiographical terms, we see this quest as a donning of masks to investigate reality, of moving through the world and "across the color line," as W. E. B. DuBois declared in *The Souls of Black Folk*. This contrapuntal movement involved, on the one hand, an attempt to immerse himself discreetly in white culture at Ohio State, and, on the other, an attempt to subvert white culture more radically, in a dialectical sense, through its soft underbelly, through crime.

By the summer of 1928, at the age of nineteen, Himes was hustling, gambling, pimping, smoking opium, committing burglaries, and stealing cars. At a party, he met his first wife, Jean Johnson, whom he would marry eight years later and live with for fourteen years. He was arrested for weapons theft and received a suspended sentence. Journeying to Columbus in a stolen car, he began passing bad checks while associating with his old university friends. Arrested a second time, he spent until November in the county jail; when his case came to trial, he again was given a two-year suspended sentence. By the end of November, he was arrested in Chicago for a $53,000 armed robbery in the first degree. On 27 December 1928, Himes was sentenced to twenty to twenty-five years of hard labor in the Ohio State Penitentiary.

Prison Life

In a generic pattern common to the *Autobiography* of Malcolm X and other narratives by black Americans, Himes came to maturity and adult consciousness while in prison: "I grew to manhood in Ohio State Penitentiary. I was nineteen years old when I went in and twenty-six years old when I came out. I became a man, dependent on no one but myself. I learned all the behavior patterns necessary for survival, or I wouldn't have survived, although at the time I did not realize I was learning them"(60). Yet even Himes's prison identity is provisional, not yet complete, for what he encountered in prison—violence, sexuality, racism, and neurotic behavior—was little more than he had encountered outside. His new identity, nevertheless, began to take shape when he discovered his true role as a writer.

Himes found and defined himself in prison through writing. In fact, his education and his reputation as a published author of stories and crime fiction in *Atlanta World, Abbott's Monthly,* and *Esquire* in the early 1930s conveyed a degree of status that permitted Himes to survive prison politics.[7] Within the autobiographical process of *The Quality of Hurt,* we also see the fictional process of writing one's life, for Himes's early fiction—notably the superlative "To What Red Hell," based on the Easter Monday fire of 1930 at the penitentiary in which 330 convicts were burned to death, published in *Esquire* in 1935—came close to the plot of his personal experience.

Embedded in Himes's autobiographical narrative is the record of a man coming to artistic consciousness. Gradually we become aware that long before he began to write his autobiography toward the end of his life, Himes had been living a life and writing about it through fiction. Unlike Malcolm X, who converted to Islam, Himes converts to the role of artist—of a writer in opposition, based on his recognition that America would conspire to oppress him unless he conspired successfully in turn to be what he wanted to be, a writer, at any cost—even expatriation. Ultimately prison life became a metaphor for the entire American experience and for fictive protagonists who where badly concealed avatars of Himes's own experience of racial hurt in the 1930s and 1940s.

Released from prison in 1936 and soon married to Jean, Himes discovered that although he was not firmly in control of his life, his development as a writer provided a structuring principle for his passage through contemporary events. Whether working as a writer on the Ohio Writer's Project, moving through a series of twenty-three jobs in Los Angeles in the early 1940s, living on a rundown farm owned by his brother-in-law in northern California, or hopping from city to country in the New York metropolitan area between 1944 and 1952, Himes attempts through a welter of episodic material to convey an exemplary life as a dedicated writer: "No matter what I did, or where I was, or how I lived, I had considered myself a writer ever since I'd published my first story in *Esquire* when I was still in prison in 1934. Foremost a writer. Above all else a writer. It was my salvation, and is. The world can deny me all other employment, and stone me as an ex-convict, as a nigger, as a disagreeable and unpleasant person. But as long as I write, whether it is published or not, I'm a writer, and no one can take that away" (117). Himes captures here the life-shaping power of an artistic vocation designed at least in part to subdue the latent absurdities and hurts that had become the fundamental fact of existence for him in the United States.

Given this need to validate a life through art, it is evident that Himes would attempt a personal coloration of his fiction. A first long novel, *Black Sheep*, started in 1937 and completed in 1939 while Himes was staying on author Louis Bromfield's Malabar Farm in Pleasant Valley, Ohio, was based on his prison experience. Accepted initially by Holt, it was rejected at the last minute by Ted Amussen, the managing editor. (Himes ultimately would retitle the manuscript *Cast the First Stone* and get it published in 1952.) Himes's first published novels, *If He Hollers Let Him Go* (1945) and *Lonely Crusade* (1947), illuminate the author's private perceptions of World War II Los Angeles as the epitome of America's racist culture. His semiautobiographical *The Third Generation* (1954) focuses closely on the history of the Bomar family. An affair with Vandi Haygood, acting director of fellowships for the Rosenwald Foundation during World War II, provided the substance of *The Primitive* (1955). Thus, Himes's fiction can be treated in part as a single autobiographical text. From the very earliest phase of his writing, the private self of Chester Himes, the autobiographical element, is part of the complex relationship that his protagonists have with the prison house of American culture.

Expatriation

The indomitable reality of American culture and the need of Chester Himes to transcend it led to his departure from the United States on 3 April 1953 aboard the *Ile de France*. A year earlier, Paris reviewers had chosen *Lonely Crusade*, translated into French, as one of the five most important American books published in France. Although now in the company of Wouk, Hemingway, Fitzgerald, and Faulkner in France, Himes had received terrible reviews in the United States for *Lonely Crusade*. Facing hostile critics and the dissolution of his marriage at home, as well as tensions transmitted by American culture, Himes determined to shape his personal and artistic experience anew as an expatriate. On 11 April Himes arrived at Le Havre, having started an affair with Mrs. Alva Trent Van Olden Barneveldt (a pseudonym for Mrs. Willa Thompson), a Philadelphia heiress. He was forty-three.

Whereas book 1 of *The Quality of Hurt* had compressed the first forty-three years of Himes's life into a cosmology framed by the need of its creator to find an authentic voice through art, books 2 and 3 of the first volume of the autobiography offer a more leisurely and coherent view of the first year and a half of the author's expatriation in Europe. Here Himes explores a universe where the chasms separating himself from culture can be analyzed from a new perspective. Although provisionally accepted by Parisian artistic society, Himes quickly perceived the persistent anomalies in the biracial social structure, including the status of the black American subculture.

Richard Wright, whom Himes had known in New York, helped the author to locate accommodations in Paris and get his cultural bearings. Nevertheless, Himes intentionally minimized both the presence of Wright in his life during this first year of expatriation, as well as his contact with other black expatriates. Concerning Wright, Baldwin, and other black expatriates, Himes finds it difficult to express a single retrospective thought that is not touched with irony. For example, when Wright misses Himes's arrival by train in Paris and searches desperately for him, Himes observes: "As all his friends knew, Dick had an excitable temperament and was given to such self-indulgent exaggeration that the buzzing of a blowfly could range like a typhoon in his imagination"(177). Similarly, when Wright catches up with Himes the next morning and takes him to the Café Monaco for breakfast, Himes writes: "Dick greeted everyone with boisterous condescension; it was obvious he was the King thereabouts"(179). Just as his life in America had existed in counterpoint to a hostile culture, Himes consciously wills himself to begin life in Paris on a note of disharmony, disconnecting himself from the people and groups surrounding him.

The alienation of Chester Himes and his awareness of it is an intimate part of his autobiographical journey toward self-knowledge. His self-oriented universe, his world of experience, is dominated by conflict; it is the pivot of his emotional and artistic life. We sense this existential and rhetorical strategy in his classic description of an encounter between Wright and James Baldwin at the Deux Magots:

I was somewhat surprised to find Baldwin a small, intense young man of great excitability. Dick started right off needling Baldwin, who defended himself with such intensity that he stammered, his body trembled, and his face quivered. I sat and worked from one to the other, Dick playing the fat cat and forcing Baldwin into the role of the quivering mouse. It wasn't particularly funny, but then Dick wasn't a funny man. I never found it easy to laugh with Dick; it was far easier to laugh at him on occasion. Dick accused Baldwin of showing his gratitude for all he had done for him by his scurrilous attacks. Baldwin defended himself by saying that Dick had written his story and hadn't left him, or any other American black writer, anything to write about. (201)

Whether reporting on encounters with black Americans, French artists, or publishers, Himes retains a detached bemusement as part of his persona. Nevertheless, in moments of candor, Himes must defend Wright—and only Richard Wright—as a great man, a greater writer, and a friend: "Whatever his faults and deficiencies, Richard Wright was the first American black writer to break into the big time, and by so doing he had convinced the world that it was possible for the American black descendants of slaves to possess the talent and the intellectual capacity to contribute to the world's literature" (211).

No matter how insular he considers himself, Himes unavoidably connects personal lives and relationships to the broader cultural fabric. St. Clair Drake has commented on this distinctive element in black autobiography: "The genre is one in which more intimate aspects of the autobiographer's personal experience are subordinates to social commentary and reflections on what it means to be a Negro in a world dominated by white men. There have been no black Marcel Prousts and André Gides. The traumatic effects of the black experience have made confessional writing an intellectual luxury black writers cannot afford."[8] With Himes, we are constantly aware that autobiographical consciousness embraces both the author's recollections about his life—rendered in far more intimate detail than St. Clair Drake might acknowledge—and the distinctive phenomenon of reflected social consciousness. Himes's "true" story of himself, designed to illuminate "the quality of hurt" in his life, is conterminous with his insights into culture. Painful recollections are not self-indulgent but rather recurring metaphors of a self attempting to achieve liberation in a culture, a world, that would deny him authentic freedom.

At the same time, Himes does not subsume his intimate personal voice to any lengthy discourses on history. In fact, he inflates rather than minimizes himself in order to assert his place in the world. We perceive not only the "organic reality of the person" but also the "growth of a person in a cultural milieu."[9] Perhaps Ralph Ellison, whom Himes had met and liked when he first came to New York and whom he invited to Wading River in late 1946, captures this coincidence of personality and culture best. In his essay on Richard Wright's *Black Boy*, Ellison alludes to its blues tonalities, sensing in the novel "an impulse to keep the painful details and episodes of a brutal experience alive in one's aching consciousness, to finger its jagged grain, and to transcend it, not by the consolation of philosophy but by squeezing from it a near-tragic, near-comic lyricism."[10] Similarly, with Himes's autobiography, we sense the seriocomic elements that render his total existence in terms of the blues.

The Quality of Hurt

One of the great strengths of the blues is its adaptability, the skill with which it absorbs the sounds and rhythms of pain, evolving into a love affair with life. Alva's arrival in Europe, constituting the thematic focus of the third part of *The Quality of Hurt*, is the blues note that makes Himes realize, as he wrote much later on 6 June 1971 in Alicante, Spain, the "desperate struggle for life" that erases even hurt. In Alva, Himes discovers another human being "so very hurt by life"(162) that even he, suspicious and cynical, must recognize her as part of himself.

Himes's love affair with Alva, which covers almost 200 pages, is another major turning point in his life. Affronted by Richard Wright's flippant dismissal of this fragile, timid, emotionally bruised white woman of forty, Himes leaves Paris with Alva for Arcachon, on the Bay of Biscay, in the summer of 1953. Some of the brightest, most chromatic writing in the autobiography covers their odyssey of love and despair from Arcachon, where they spent two months; to London from July through December 1953; to Mallorca in January 1954; and to Paris, where Himes sent Alva back via ship to the United States on 1 December 1954.

Writing of this affair, Himes rarely reverts to cynical counterpoint. Even his descriptions of their rapturous sexual interludes, in which they lose themselves in each other, lack the chauvinistic cynicism that characterizes Himes's earlier treatment of his sexual history. In fact, Himes acknowledges an abiding love for Alva even when he recognizes that "she just wanted to lose her identity in the soft exquisite darkness of sensuality, which was all [he] had become to her" (300). There is an almost elegiac feeling for Alva: "No white man has ever felt more protective toward his wife than I toward Alva. And yet I felt an enormous, moving pity for her that she had given up her place in the white world for me"(301). From the initial sexual bond that united them aboard the *Ile de France*, Himes moves in the latter pages of *The Quality of Hurt* to a stoic defense of their love that transcends race, gender, and culture.

Despite persistent insolvency, Himes and Alva take an almost fairy-tale pleasure in themselves as transcontinental waifs, enduring personal and public hurts. They seem to write ceaselessly, Himes collaborating with Alva on their 520-page manuscript *The Golden Chalice* and also writing *The End of the Primitive*, a novel that not uncoincidentally traces an affair between an American black man and a white woman. When Alva and Himes stop working and their typewriter falls silent, their relationship, too, is in hiatus. When New American Library offers Himes a $1,000 advance for *The Primitive*, he uses the money to pay debts and send Alva back to the United States. "But what about me? I asked myself, where could I find that was safe?"(351). With a prophetic note of uncertainty, Chester Himes ends the first volume of his autobiography in the forty-fifth year of his life in an intermediate area— disconnected from Alva and prepared to reconstruct once again his capricious life.

The Dialectics of Absurdity

From the first volume of the autobiography of Chester Himes emerges the figure of a person who opposes American culture and senses the grotesque nuances of his world. In the second volume, *My Life of Absurdity*, Himes perceives more clearly his antipathy toward culture as an outgrowth of the absurd instability Western civilization creates for all black men and women. His philosophy as an artist, in which he sees Western culture dominated by the doctrine of racism, is shaped increasingly by a recognition that his own absurd life had become a picaresque adventure across international borders.

Himes deliberately positions himself as an absurd protagonist at the outset of the second volume of his autobiography:

Albert Camus once said that racism is absurd. Racism introduces absurdity into the human condition. Not only does racism express the absurdity of the racists, but it generates absurdity in the victims. And the absurdity of the victims intensifies the absurdity of the racists, ad infinitum. If one lives in a country where racism is held valid and practiced in all ways of life, eventually, no matter whether one is a racist or a victim, one comes to feel the absurdity of life.

Racism generating from whites is first of all absurd. Racism creates absurdity among blacks as a defense mechanism. Absurdity to combat absurdity.[11]

Burning against culture's restrictions, Himes as arch-bohemian in Paris in the 1950s and 1960s casts himself in the persona of absurd hero and absurd artist. He becomes a new type of literary subversive who probes the comic incongruities and tragic absurdities of "civilization." He is now the crusader against racial prejudice in his flamboyance, garrulousness, and licentiousness. To recognize the absurd is, as Camus indicates in *The Myth of Sisyphus*, to become a rebel.

Himes also perceives his fiction as locked in a dialectic of absurdity. Speaking in the second volume of his autobiography of *The Primitive* (1954), also published as *La Fin d'un primitif (The end of the primitive)* by Editions Gallimard in 1957, Himes places both the text and himself in the world of the absurd: "The first time I read the manuscript of my novel *The End of the*

Primitive, I knew I had written an absurd book. But it had not been my intention to write about absurdity. I had intended to write about the deadly
venom of racial prejudice which kills both racists and their victims. I had not
intended to write about absurdity because the book was about me and I had
not known at the time that I was absurd"(1). *The Primitive*, which Himes for
some time considered his best novel, is exceedingly pessimistic in its semiautobiographical tracing of the failed interracial love affair between Jesse and
Kriss. At the same time, elements of absurdity infuse Himes's brooding dis-
enchantment with culture.

James Lundquist notes the ambivalent and conflicting demands of absurdity in his assessment of *The Primitive*: "To mention humor at all in discussing a novel that ends with a drunken murder scene seems macabre, but
The Primitive, while tragic in outline, is filled with incidents and conversa-
tions that are handled with Rabelaisian gusto. Gargantuan eating and drink-
ing scenes are described in a style that effectively blends the high and low." [12]
The contrary strains of tragedy and comedy that unite in the art of absurdity
capture the psychic stress and cultural tensions, the divisive emotional states,
that characterize Himes's fiction and his autobiography.

A man who for a lifetime has been buffeted by hazards, bludgeoned by
racism, disenchanted by resistance to his writing, obsessed with sex and by
the folly of his numerous affairs with women, is attuned existentially to the
absurd contours of life. As absurd hero, Himes expresses his major mission:
"I had come to a final decision a long time ago when I was in prison that I was
going to live as long as possible to aggravate the white race"(13). Thus Himes
is seen in his autobiography as a figure who through the transcription of his
life registers keenly the warring elements in culture that make the black condition absurd: "I saw the life of a black man as an absurdity"(101).

Black expatriates in Paris in the 1950s seemed to exist in the robust and
skeptical world of the absurd. Gathering at the Café Tournon, they were intent on creating an environment of unconventional and cynical amusement
for themselves. Here at the café, which became by 1956 a tourist mecca,
there were Richard Wright, loving and loathing his bourgeois life; Ollie
Harrington, the creator of "Bootsie" in the *Pittsburgh Courier*; Bertel, the
painter from Gary, Indiana; Frank Van Bracken, Paris correspondent for *Eb-
ony*; the artist Walter Coleman; Ish Kelley, the prototype for Fish Belly in
Wright's *The Long Dream*; William Gardner Smith; and other members of
the black colony. And surrounding them were white women, actresses in the
passion play that unfolded nightly at Café Tournon. Himes observes: "I never
met an American black man at that time in Paris who wasn't living with one
or more white women or married to one" (34).

Remembering the ambiance of the Café Tournon, Himes captures some of the conflicting patterns of feeling in his life in this paragraph:

The evenings I went to the Café Tournon and exchanged jokes with Ollie. In front of that vast white audience I could not restrain myself any more than he could. We were fantastically absurd, all of us blacks. Ollie was funny. I could always follow Ollie's lead. The absurdity of two other blacks was ofttimes hurting. But ours never, it was only entertaining. During that spring the Café Tournon became the most celebrated café in all of Europe, and from there one could select entertainments of all types. All of us vocal blacks collected there to choose our white woman for each night, and the white women gathered about us and waited our selection. White women love an absurd black, especially if he's funny. (37)

Through his sense of the absurd, Himes is able to reconstruct yet another identity for himself. "My life was weird, grotesque, a drunken Walpurgisnacht," he declares. Expatriation forces Himes to reject some elements of himself and affirm others: "I knew the life of an American black needed another image than just the victim of racism. We were more than just victims. We did not suffer, we were extroverts. We were unique individuals, funny but not clowns, solemn but not serious, hurt but not suffering, sexualists but not whores in the usual sense of the word; we had a tremendous love of life, a love of sea, a love of ourselves. We were absurd" (36). By identifying this new mental constitution, Himes exposes himself to warring elements in his existence, knowing that the very irrationality and ludicrousness of his life as an expatriate ultimately will permit him to be a new type of creative artist.

"La Série noire"

"I'm the lowest-paid writer on the face of the earth," Himes once observed to novelist John Williams—yet another absurdity for the author to contend with.[13] Rarely paid more than token advances by American publishers, Himes in 1956 began writing detective stories for Marcel Duhamel, editor of Gallimard's "La Série noire." Duhamel had translated Himes's first novel, *If He Hollers Let Him Go*, into French; he offered Himes, who needed the money, a $1,000 advance to write a detective story for his series. Duhamel suggested that Himes read Raymond Chandler and Dashiell Hammett, and then produce a hard-boiled narrative of 220 pages. Beggars can't be choosers, mused Himes; he accepted Duhamel's offer. Between 1957 and 1969 he published nine novels in the detective genre that established him as a celebrated American writer in Europe, especially among intellectuals and university students.

Just as his earlier fiction had been close to his own life in plot and theme, Himes's entry into the new genre of detective fiction permitted him a more graphic and curiously more philosophical rehearsal of the horrors and absurdities of his existence and his times. Through the adventures of the black detectives, Coffin Ed Johnson and Grave Digger Jones, two high priests of violence, Himes was able to promote his explicit argument, worked out at length in fiction and autobiography, that life is essentially crazy. Roger Rosenblatt asserts, "Autobiography as a genre should be the history of individual craziness, but in black autobiography the outer reality in which heroes move is so massive and absolute in its craziness that any one person's individual idiosyncrasies seem almost dull in their normalcy."[14] With Coffin Ed and Grave Digger, Himes's helter-skelter autobiographical self decomposes and reconstitutes itself in a medium noted for its mayhem. Similarly Himes's actual "kaleidoscopic" existence at the time, centering on a latently explosive and prolonged affair with a young German woman, Marlene Behrens, augments his creative vision. Himes admits in *My Life of Absurdity*: "I was writing some strange shit. Some time before, I didn't know when, my mind had rejected all reality as I had known it and I had begun to see the world as a cesspool of buffoonery. Even the violence was funny. A man gets his throat cut. He shakes his head to say you missed me and it falls off. Damn reality, I thought. All of reality was absurd, contradictory, violent and hurting. It was funny, really. If I could just get the handle to joke. And I had got the handle, by some miracle" (126). Traveling compulsively with Marlene from Paris to Germany, to the south of France, to Denmark, to Mallorca, always back to Paris, Himes keeps himself (and a rather bizarre Volkswagen) running with grotesque energy. Yet he is happy only when writing his "strange, violent, unreal stories" that constitute the Harlem of his imagination.

Two weeks after receiving the first part of his advance, Himes returned to Duhamel with the first eighty pages of *The Five Cornered Square*, which Minnie Danzas would translate into French as *La Reine des pommes*. Based loosely on one of Walter Coleman's tall tales about a confidence game, this action story appealed to Duhamel, who gave Himes a few pointers on detective fiction and offered him another advance for a second detective novel. Returning to his room with a pocketful of money, Himes reread for inspiration his favorite novel of the absurd, Faulkner's *Sanctuary*, and then went to work again on the manuscript. He worked all Christmas Day 1956 and through New Year's Eve; on 18 January 1957 he finished his first detective novel and turned it over to Duhamel for translation. Published first in 1957 as a paperback original by Fawcett with the title *For Love of Imabelle* (and later by Avon in 1965 as *A Rage in Harlem*), it was released in Paris in 1958, winning France's coveted literary prize, the Grand prix de roman policière for the year's best detective novel.

Himes and Marlene spent part of 1957 in Denmark, where he continued to write detective fiction: "I liked writing, not only of the visual scenes, which I could always see plainly, and the dialogue, which I could hear clearly spoken, but of the thoughts which were mine in any given situation. I could think like the teen-age gangsters, the black multitude of Harlem, the black detectives" (150). In a letter to Carl Van Vechten dated 26 August Himes confesses that he was so engrossed in his crime novel *If Trouble Was Money* (based on a blues song by Bessie Smith) that he forgot daily details. By the middle of September, he had completed his second detective novel.

Reviewing his early years as a writer of detective fiction, Himes emphasizes in his autobiography the psychological and ideological contours of his new vocation:

I must confess that all during the five-year period when I was writing my first six detective stories my writing reflected my immediate state of mind; I traveled through Europe trying desperately to find a life into which I would fit; and my determination stemmed from my desire to succeed without America. . . . I went through life without liking anyone, black or white, living with a young woman whom I always suspected of infidelities and of whom I was always jealous. But my mind worked like it was on fire; I could write like a bird sings; I never had to hesitate for a word to describe my thoughts, or for a scene to record its continuity. (155)

Himes's opposition to the cultural order is basic and manifests itself in the genre of detective fiction. At the same time, we sense in the autobiography a psychic configuration between the mayhem of Himes's detective fiction and the author's own vision—his narrative—of his existence.

Himes's achieved vision in the second volume of his autobiography, his search for the meaning of his experience as a writer and person, clearly finds illumination in his evolving success as a writer of detective fiction. His is a special genre because of his black antiheroes and his Harlem settings, which permit him to reveal "the American black's secret mind itself" (158). Acknowledging in his autobiography that he received high praise for *La Reine des pommes* from Jean Cocteau, Jean Giono, and others, Himes is inclined to impute a meaning to his detective fiction that transcends the superficialities of the genre. Essentially the grotesque and violent world of Chester Himes's detective fiction is a corollary of his own immersion in a civilization that is colonialist, and hence racist, on both sides of the Atlantic. For example, while living in Mallorca with Marlene in December 1957, Himes in a letter to Carl Van Vechten offered a detailed synopsis and evaluation of a novel, *A Case of Rape* (Une Affaire de viol), that underscores the international problem of racism. In its initial conception, *A Case of Rape* is the story of five American blacks in Paris who are falsely accused of raping and murdering a white woman. In Himes's words:

The story is developed by the sixth Negro, who is a famous expatriate writer who sets out to investigate the backgrounds of each of the accused in an effort to prove that a conviction of Negro men to the charge of raping a white woman is always a political maneuver. He does not prove it. But by his search he reveals himself as a political pawn, and this makes him reevaluate his life and his work. The story is essentially the biographies of these people and the inner compulsions that have brought all their varying lives to this common focal point. (171)

As a problem in detection and perception only geographically removed from Himes's Harlem crime fiction, *A Case of Rape* constitutes the author's indictment of a civilization geared to do violence to all peoples of color, to render them not only as oppressed peoples but also as absurdities.

Fame

Returning to France in April 1958, Himes immediately received a contract from Plon for *Mamie Mason* (which also would be published by Olympia Press and publishers in England, Japan, and the United States as *Pinktoes*) and then went with Marlene to Vence on the Côte d'Azur to write. "Everything seemed to work well. We had the sea, the mountains, the bright, hot days, the cool pleasant nights" (180). Himes finished *Run Man Run* and signed another contract with Duhamel for *The Big Gold Dream*. At Duhamel's villa in Vence in July, Himes was shown the first bound copy of *La Reine des pommes*, with Giono's extravagant blurb, "I give you all of Hemingway, Dos Passos, and Fitzgerald for this Chester Himes." The next week, Himes went to Paris to receive La Grand prix du roman policier for the novel. In France, Himes had become, in his words, "a person comparable to Richard Wright" (181). He had become famous by writing detective novels about "blacks with their extreme absurdity" (182).

In March 1959, with Marlene home in Germany, Himes returned to Paris, where he began an affair with Lesley Packard, who would become his second wife. Lesley, who was Irish-English, worked as a librarian and wrote a shopping column for the Paris edition of the *New York Herald Tribune*. "She was beautiful and chic and wore fashionable clothes, was well liked and knowledgeable, altogether different from Marlene, which made me wonder why I had been with Marlene" (186). Himes was famous now in Paris and the center of attention at Le Café Touron, but he was still rejected by the American press. In September 1959 a reporter had written in the *New York Times Book Review*, "Himes is a small man with a little moustache and a big dog who has written such unsuccessful books as *The Primitive, Cast the First Stone, If He Hollers Let Him Go* and *The Third Generation* and is now writing detective stories for the French Serie Noire."[15] Hurt by this rejection, affected by the first in a series of heart seizures and a case of ulcers, Himes fought back with another absurd tale, *All Shot Up*. "I took myself seriously as a writer of absurd stories and the Americans could go to hell" (201).

Continuing his frenetic writing schedule, Himes began another book in 1960, *Be Calm*—"about Sister Heavenly, Uncle Saint, Pinky and a three-million-dollar cache of dope, and the gangsters who have lost it, which wound up many months later being called *The Heat's On* and later still as a movie called *Come Back, Charleston Blue*"(201). Himes traveled with Lesley through Italy. In November they were in St. Tropez. On 29 or 30 November the proprietor at Himes's hotel told the author that he had just heard over the radio that Richard Wright had died. Himes and Ollie Harrington were the only close friends at Wright's funeral in Paris. "It seemed," writes Himes, "as if Dick's death put an accelerator on my own life, which began to spin like a buzz saw. . . . I had never realized before how much influence Dick had over me" (217).

By 1961 Himes's fame in France had not produced financial solvency; he constantly lived with Lesley on the "edge of destitution" (229). Sufficiently well known to consort with figures such as Picasso and Malcolm X, Himes nevertheless had a singular inability to negotiate successful contracts. Small advances and freelance work barely sustained him. In 1962 he traveled to New York on assignment for *France-Soir* and ORTF to do a film documentary on Harlem. There through Lewis Michaux he met Malcolm X: "I got to know him well. He did not have to indoctrinate me into distrusting white people; I had mistrusted them all along" (247). Later that year he went to Yucatán to write *Retour en Afrique*, which would be published in 1963 in France and in 1964 in the United States as *Cotton Comes to Harlem*. Carl Van Vechten sent Himes enough money to get him out of a Merida hospital— where he had been rushed after suffering a mild stroke—and to New York for further treatment at the Neurological Institute. By early 1963 Himes had returned to Paris and Lesley.

With the Paris publications in 1963 of *Une Affair de viol, Mamie Mason,* and *Retour en Afrique,* Chester Himes achieved celebrity status in France. *Mamie Mason (Pinktoes)* took Paris by storm, its splashy red bindings on display up and down Boulevard St. Germain, the Latin Quarter, Boulevard St. Michel, and elsewhere. *Une Affair de viol,* with a postscript by the feminist Christiane Rochfort, published at the height of the Algerian War, caused a sensation of another kind, with many French reviewers perceiving the republic as attacked by Himes for its racism. "What kept worrying me was that I was famous but broke," Himes wrote. "Everyone in Paris either knew me or knew of me and here I was, broke all the time" (275).

In 1965, shortly after a laudatory article by René Micha in the February issue of *Les Temps modernes,* entitled "Les Paroissiens de Chester Himes," the author's fortunes changed. With $10,000 in advance royalties from American publishers, Himes was relatively solvent. In Athens, he finished proofreading the manuscript of *Cotton Comes to Harlem,* which Putnam's would publish in the fall. Following sojourns in Copenhagen, Egypt, and La Ciotat between 1965 and 1966, Himes and Lesley settled in a farmhouse in Vanelles, a country village outside Aix in the south of France. Pleased with his life of newfound luxury, Himes fell into a routine of vigorous physical activity but very little writing, aside from work on his autobiography. When on 20 October 1966, Samuel Goldwyn, Jr., picked up an option on six detective stories containing Grave Digger and Coffin Ed, Chester Himes finally attained a measure of financial security that had eluded him for almost sixty years. Thanks to Hollywood, fortune caught up belatedly with Himes's European fame.

The Heat's Off

In 1970, at the height of demand for black films, *Cotton Comes to Harlem,* directed by Ossie Davis and starring Godfrey Cambridge and Raymond St. Jacques, was released by United Artists and enjoyed national success. By then, Chester and Lesley Himes were living in a house they had built in Moraira, Spain, a fishing village about ten kilometers south of Javea. Himes, now sixty-one, flew to Paris for a private screening of the film and for a round of interviews with reporters from *Le Monde, Life,* and other journals. Traveling from Paris to Germany to New York (where he met author Maya Angelou) to London, Himes ushered in the 1970s with a whirlwind itinerary that left him "feeling more confused than ever before" in his life and anxious to return to Moraira.

At Moraira Himes focused his remaining creative energy on completing his autobiography, which he had started in the 1960s. In a 29 November 1961 letter to Carl Van Vechten reprinted in *My Life of Absurdity*, Himes had rehearsed his early conception of the autobiography. "I would like very much to write this account of my years in Europe as a straight autobiography in three books; each book about my life with a woman, all three completely different; the first an American socialite (Boston-Smith College, etc.), married, divorced, three daughters; the second an infantile, immature, very crazy German in her twenties; the third English, good family, in her thirties, a member of the right people" (252). Ultimately Himes would encompass all of his life—both the American and European experience—in two volumes. The women would hover over his autobiographical landscape, from his austere class-conscious mother to his second wife, who cared for Himes as his health declined precipitously in the last ten years of his life.

By the 1980s, contending with another stroke and Parkinson's disease, Himes had good days and bad, as Lesley remarked in a conversation with John Williams. When Himes died on 12 November 1984 in Moraira, he was seventy-five years old. The brief obituary in *Publishers Weekly* captured the irony of his life and career: "*Cotton Comes to Harlem* and the six other novels featuring two black detectives in Harlem are widely rated in Europe as on a par with the works of Dashiell Hammett and Georges Simenon. Praised too are novels dealing with racism, including *If He Hollers Let Him Go* and *Lonely Crusade*."[16] Himes's work was available throughout Europe; none was in print in the United States. As the protagonist of *If He Hollers Let Him Go* had observed prophetically: "If I couldn't live in America as an equal in the minds, hearts and souls of all white people, if I couldn't know that I had a chance to do anything any other American could, to go as high as American citizenship would carry anybody, there'd never be anything in the country anyway" (186). For Chester Himes, who had always wanted to be taken seriously by his American audience, this was the lasting absurdity.

Chapter Two
California on Parade:
If He Hollers Let Him Go and *Lonely Crusade*

In the first two published novels of Chester Himes, *If He Hollers Let Him Go* (1945) and *Lonely Crusade* (1947), Los Angeles is the embodiment of the American dream transformed into grotesque nightmare. It is the manifest destiny of the protagonists in those novels, Bob Jones and Lee Gordon, to discover that any nascent sense of promise engendered by life in the City of Angels ends instead in a sense of violence, anarchy, and the absurd. Los Angeles, the Dream Factory, plays tricks on its two dreamers in these novels, even as it had played tricks on Himes.

Between 1937 and 1939, Himes had worked as a laborer, research assistant, and writer for the Works Progress Administration (WPA) in Cleveland. He had completed his long prison novel, *Black Sheep*, but publishers did not want it. With the start of American involvement in World War II, the WPA effort came to an end, and Himes was out of work. He petitioned his parole board for restoration of his citizenship and shortly after receiving it went to live on Bromfield's Malabar Farm in Pleasant Valley, Ohio. Bromfield read the first version of Himes's prison novel, liked it, and thought it had cinematic potential. Bromfield himself was going to Hollywood to work on the film adaptation of Hemingway's *For Whom the Bell Tolls*, and he volunteered to submit Himes's manuscript for consideration. He took the book with him and gave it to some producers, and Himes followed him to California.

Following a generation of writers—James M. Cain, John O'Hara, Nathanael West, F. Scott Fitzgerald, William Faulkner—Himes came to California as an outsider. Lured by the promise of cinematic success, Himes discovered instead a city in wartime that was more virulently racist than any environment he had encountered in Ohio. Even with Bromfield's support and a list of names provided by Langston Hughes of people to see, Himes had to work first in the San Francisco shipyards and then at more than twenty jobs in essential industries in Los Angeles during the first three years of the war.

The sense of extreme estrangement Himes felt in California is captured in this paragraph from *The Quality of Hurt*: "Los Angeles hurt me racially as much as any city I have ever known—much more than any city I remember from the South. It was the lying hypocrisy that hurt me. Black people were treated much the same as they were in an industrial city of the South. They were Jim-Crowed in housing, in employment, in public accommodations, such as hotels and restaurants. During the filming of *Cabin in the Sky*, starring Ethel Waters, Bill 'Bojangles' Robinson and Lena Horne, the black actors and actresses were refused service in the MGM commissary where everyone ate" (74). At one point, Himes was optimistic about doing a profile on Lena Horne for *Colliers*, but the assignment was given to a white writer. He was promised a job in the reading department at Warner Brothers until one day Jack Warner declared to a subordinate, "I don't want no niggers on this lot."[1] Himes worked at menial jobs while his wife, Jean, was employed as codirector of women's activities for the Los Angeles–area United Service Organizations. Stung by his wife's ability to find professional work while he had to take day labor, Himes senses the ultimate demolition of his marriage. He admits, "It was from the accumulation of my racial hurts that I wrote my bitter novel of protest *If He Hollers Let Him Go*" (*The Quality of Hurt*, 75).

The Dream Factory

Los Angeles in *If He Hollers Let Him Go* is a microcosm of American racial disorder. This anarchic urban landscape, set in the summer of 1942, seems to belie California's endless sunshine, even as it undercuts Bob Jones's dream of a better life. Los Angeles, as Nathanael West wrote trenchantly in *The Day of the Locust*, is the "dream dump." The bizarre dreams that afflict the main character in Himes's novel, Bob Jones, define his relationship to an equally nightmarish culture.

Bob Jones, the first-person narrator in the novel, is a prototype of the central characters whom Himes would develop in his early fiction: educated, middle class, intellectual by bent, skeptical by temperament, attuned to the logical absurdities of being black men in a racist culture. Clearly he is an avatar of Chester Himes, who wrote in a letter to John Williams, "One day I went up to get a job in the Richmond Shipyards (Henry J. Kaiser yards). From working there and later in the Los Angeles Shipyard in San Pedro harbor I got the material for IF HE HOLLERS LET HIM GO. I worked at Richmond as a shipfitter, living in SF and commuting; and I watched the growth of prejudice in San Francisco and Oakland as the tremendous influx of southern white and Negro workers poured into the area."[2]

After two years of college education in Ohio, Jones has journeyed to California, secured a job as leaderman at the Atlas Shipyard, and embarked on an affair with Alice Harrison, a casework supervisor in the city welfare department and the light-skinned daughter of the prominent Dr. Wellington L-P Harrison, described by the narrator as "a pompous little guy whom you'd expect to have a hyphenated name."[3] Jones is a boarder in the home of a working-class family, Henry and Ella Mae Brown. With Ella Mae, Jones has been on intimate terms. The contrast between this "full-bodied, slow-motioned home girl with a broad flat face, flat-nosed and thick lipped" (4) and the demure, sophisticated Alice who can pass as white, is one measure of the numerous racial ambiguities, the problems of class and caste, thrust upon him since his arrival in Los Angeles in the fall of 1941.

In the aftermath of Pearl Harbor, racism in Los Angeles floats in the air like a malignant cloud. Racism has crept into Bob Jones's consciousness in a way it never had in Cleveland. It blows into his very dreams, turning them into bizarre nightmares. In fact, the entire plot of *If He Hollers Let Him Go* is structured around five nightmarish days in Jones's life—a typical work week running from Monday to Friday. Every morning the protagonist awakes from ludicrous racial nightmares into the even more ominous racist absurdities and anomalies of actual life in Los Angeles. For example, Jones has witnessed Little Riki Oyana singing "God Bless America" and then being sent to the Japanese-American concentration camp at Santa Anita the next day. He imagines that this too could happen to him, and he senses a racist apocalypse: "It was the look in the white people's faces when I walked down the streets. It was that crazy, wild-eyed, unleashed hatred that the first Jap bomb on Pearl Harbor let loose in a flood. All that tight, crazy feeling of race as thick in the street as gas fumes" (4). Fueled by racism, life in wartime Los Angeles is chaotic, violent, schizophrenic, engendering predictably in Jones a state of angry, fearful, almost volcanic consciousness.

The urban landscape that Jones drives through daily in his 1942 Buick Roadmaster, the symbol of his middle-class aspirations, is as sharp and brittle as his consciousness. It assaults him, contributing to his state of imminent explosion: "Now I felt the heat of the day, saw the hard bright California sunshine. It lay in the road like a white frozen brilliance, hot but unshimmering, cutting the vision of my eyes into unwavering curves and stark unbroken angles" (45). Nature itself seems to be ominously and eternally white: "The vertical sun had a hard California brilliance, powder-white and eye-searing" (197). These metaphoric images, strikingly similar to those in Camus's *The Stranger*, capture a protagonist utterly alienated from his environment, mildly deracinated by the monochromatic assault on his consciousness. From

San Pedro to Main Street downtown to Little Tokyo to the harbor road, radiating outward in all directions, Los Angeles lies beneath a fierce white dream. Nature itself, as well as the cluttered streets that Jones races and rages through in his Buick, contributes to the sense of anarchy and oppression governing his life.

The Outsider

Compressed into five days, the narrative of *If He Hollers Let Him Go* is a distilled archetypal history of injustices filtered through the mind of Bob Jones, whose conventional name is the symbol of an almost invisible identity in dominant white culture. As Jones confronts persistently the contours of racist southern California culture, he too assumes the stature of representative black man attempting to escape the degradation and oppression that seems culturally predestined for him. Twice an outsider—by geography and race—he is constantly reviled by whites and blacks of lower, lateral, and higher economic and social status.

The fate predestined for this outsider is embodied in the refrain from a traditional children's counting game that gives the novel its title:

> Eenie meenie miney mo
> Catch a nigger by the toe
> If he hollers let him go
> Out goes Y-O-U.

Himes's novel is framed by this racist ditty, and in a sense it also controls the absurd attempts of its hero, or antihero, to be caught, to be hurled beyond or "outside" the domain of white culture that he must make his pilgrim's progress through.

One of the many ironic qualities of *If He Hollers Let Him Go* is Jones's ambiguous status of being simultaneously immersed in white culture and yet outside it in the sense that people would deny him an authentic personal identity. The Los Angeles roads and highways that Jones travels each morning and afternoon to and from work, more than forty miles in all, give a unique rhythm of immersion and invisibility to the novel's protagonist. The fine June weather means nothing to Bob Jones, who must engage in actual and figurative combat simply to get himself and his black coworkers to Atlas. These symbolic rides are primal episodes in racial consciousness. The highways become spatial expressions not only of Los Angeles life but also of a social structure rooted in racism. In one early morning episode, for instance, Bob Jones encounters a typical situation:

It never failed, every time I got in a hurry I got caught by every light. I pulled up in the outside lane, abreast a V-8 and an Olds, shifted back to first, and got set to take the lead. When the light turned green it caught a white couple in the middle of the street. The V-8 full of white guys dug off and started to run for it; and the two white guys in the Olds blasted at them with the horn, making them jump like grasshoppers. But when they looked up and saw we were colored they just took their time, giving us a look of cold hatred. (15)

Here the very Los Angeles roads that swallow and spit out Bob Jones are the expression of a particular urban pathology.

From the primary morning episodes of parodic movement along Los Angeles's highways, in which Bob Jones's "freedom" is undercut by his bondage to white motorists, pedestrians, and police, he moves to a more profound alienation and isolation as a worker at Atlas Shipyards. The very ship within which Jones and the black workers he supervises live is a microcosm of the social, economic, and political structures designed to keep them in a state of perpetual servitude. They are employed only because President Roosevelt's wartime directive mandates American industry to end discriminatory hiring practices. In fact, token integration in industry during World War II occurred only after A. Phillip Randolph had threatened a march on Washington. Nevertheless, Jones and his coworkers are segregated and given the worst assignments within the racist shipyard. Himes renders superbly the crammed, labyrinthine quarters on the third deck where Jones's black crew is working on the ventilation system: "The air was so thick with welding fumes, acid smell, body odor, and cigarette smoke even the stream from the blower couldn't get it out. I had fifteen in my gang, twelve men and three women, and they were all working in the tiny cramped quarters. Two firepots were going, heating soldering irons. Somebody was drilling. Two or three guys were hand-riveting. A chipper was working on the deck above. It was stifling hot, and the din was terrific" (24). Halfway between bedlam and hell, these foul quarters contribute to Jones's transient state of being. Within the ship yet displaced from it, Jones as a lower-level supervisor must fight continually for the simple prerogatives—access to blueprints, for example—that his white counterparts take for granted.

At work, Jones's consciousness is on hair trigger. He is alert to systematic racist slights and assaults by white workers and supervisors and prepared to confront this racism. Noel Schraufnagel aptly describes Jones as a "metaphysical rebel" in his intellectual awareness of his condition, but he is also a political rebel in the tradition of Camus, carrying with him an awareness that his rebellion must persist even in the face of inevitable defeat.[4] Bob has to contend with a white supervisor, Kelly, who resents Jones's promotion to leaderman. On the first workday of the week, Jones tries to recruit a white woman worker named Madge as a tracker, but she asserts that she will not work for a "nigger." In response, Jones calls her a "cracker bitch"; hauled before the superintendent, MacDougal, he is informed that he will be demoted to mechanic the following week and reclassified 1-A. The dualities and dislocations caused by race make Jones's situation strictly absurd.

That afternoon, Jones finds himself an outsider once again while participating in a crap game with a dozen or so white workers and two black workers. When he wins at dice, the white workers accuse him of cheating, and one, a tall blond named Johnny Stoddart, hits him from behind and knocks him out. A loser even when winning, Jones senses that rebellion against this paradoxical condition is his only destiny. Subsequently he stalks Stoddart at work and even follows him to his house in Huntington Park, instilling in the white man the same conscious fear and powerlessness that Jones himself contends with every day.

Despite his racial anxiety and anger, his deracinated state, and what Edward Margolies terms his "deep castration fears" that have "psychologically emasculated" him, Jones resents racist manipulation.[5] Margolies faults *If He Hollers Let Him Go* for its tediousness and lack of progression. In reality, the novel has the verve and drive of the tough-guy fiction of the thirties and forties, as well as the critical social analysis that characterizes this tradition. Jones as outsider and rebel must persistently fight for a vision of self-possession in a world geared to denying him any form of empowerment. The novel is indeed about power—from the workplace to Main Street—and Jones's understanding of who rules America is cumulative as he moves frenetically through the corruption of life in Los Angeles.

Race, Class, and Sex

The Los Angeles that presents itself to Bob Jones is a study in class and caste conflict. Jones's migratory nature takes him through multiple social strata of Los Angeles society. Even as the social landscape changes, Jones retains his dual identity as an intense participant in events and an observer of a hostile world. Embedded in this urban wanderer's consciousness is a specific knowledge of distinctions based on race, class, caste, and gender.

Jones's peregrinations in Los Angeles force him to confront a social landscape in conflict and disarray. For instance, he stays away from Atlas on Tuesday and begins his day downtown in Little Tokyo—a psychic continuation of his nightmare that night in which he was lying in a street downtown, being beaten by two white men. This is an underworld area, populated by "spooks and spills," a magnet for armed services personnel, a racial amalgam of blacks, whites, and Mexican-Americans driven by visceral needs. In a hotel bar near First and San Pedro, he watches a potentially volatile ritual unfold as a white southern girl who has come in with two white sailors flirts with the black patrons: "I thought hopefully, well, here it goes . . . if there was any kind of rumpus with the white chick in it, there wouldn't be any way at all to stop a riot-—the white GIs would swarm into Little Tokyo like they did in the Mexican districts during the zoot suit riots" (92). Himes himself had been witness to the Los Angeles zoot suit riots of 1943 and had written about the episode, finding in it another emblem of America's racial dislocation.[6] In *If He Hollers Let Him Go*, Himes has his protagonist wish for a riot, or, better, a Japanese triumph, in order to hasten the collapse of a culture where the racial and class disparities are too acute.

Jones's subversive, potentially nihilistic vision of class and caste extends dramatically to his relationship with Alice Harrison. The Harrisons live on the west side, the Beverly Hills for black citizens, removed from the black ghetto on the south side. They are emblematic of the black elite. Mrs. Harrison takes her gospel on the "negro problem" from Booker T. Washington and Eleanor Roosevelt; Dr. Harrison, "one of the richest Negroes in the city if not the whole west coast" (10), is a lecherous, dried-up man in his late sixties whom Himes satirizes viciously. Alice, whom Jones's affectionate landlady, Ella Mae, terms "the whitest colored girl you could find" (47), is a high society deb. She has, as a casework supervisor, superficial social concerns. Frequently crossing the margins of black and white culture, harboring complex libidinal drives that Himes hints might reflect a latent lesbianism, she nevertheless can love Bob Jones if she succeeds in getting him back to the university and remolding him in her image of a black professional.

Bob's powerful, assertive blackness, however, is an embarrassment to Alice. When he takes her to an exclusive, traditionally segregated high society downtown restaurant, she is mortified to be seen with a man who is palpably black. They are seated near the kitchen door and served begrudgingly in this bastion of "solid white America," and when they receive the bill, there are two typed lines added: *"We served you this time but we do not want your patronage in the future"* (73). Whether in the seediest or most exclusive parts of Los Angeles, images of cultural conflict force Jones's consciousness into a state of persistent tension.

Alice would have Bob intellectualize and objectify his problems, and indeed those of all black Americans. When he visits the Harrison house and encounters Alice and three female friends intensely discussing the problems that confront the social worker in Little Tokyo, Jones is repelled by their "cut-rate jive in social worker's phraseology that proved a certain intellectualism" (101). When pushed for an answer to Los Angeles's racial problems, he is sardonic and, again, apocalyptic: "Well now, I think we ought to kill the colored residents and eat them. In that way we'll not only solve the race problem but alleviate the race problem as well" (101). Again, when Alice's white coworker arrives and they begin to discuss *Native Son*, Bob takes an iconoclastic view of the protagonist Bigger Thomas in Wright's novel and asserts that the only solution to the Negro problem is revolution. When they are alone, Alice chides Jones for being boorish and antisocial. She loves him but wants him to apologize to the worker whom he has insulted, Madge Perkins.

Jones is trapped in a menacing triangle involving Alice, who would domesticate him, and Madge, who would have him lynched. Himes depicts Madge in the heightened grotesque contours of "pure white Texas." Madge, crude and uneducated, is a sexual and racial threat: "She had a sign up in front of her as high as Civic Center—KEEP AWAY, NIGGERS, I'M WHITE!" (152). She is doubly dangerous because she finds black men sexually attractive even as she loathes them. She is a professional disaster for a man like Jones. Nevertheless, leading life on the edge, he embraces her menacing presence. He visits her in her apartment on Fiquerosa, and in a primal confrontation Madge urges him to rape her, an invitation that actually drains him of passion. He escapes her destructive contrivances the first time but unintentionally is trapped by Madge in a second encounter the next day, Thursday.

Although his mind keeps rebelling against the image of the well-adjusted black professional that Alice would create for him, Jones nevertheless proposes to her on Thursday. He then apologizes to his supervisor MacDougal, trying to get his old job back, but is told that first he must prove his tractability by working under a white leaderman, Tebbel. While checking out a new job, he inadvertently stumbles upon Madge, who is sleeping on a bunk in an unused room. He attempts to leave but, hearing footsteps, retreats to the room, and Madge locks him in. When a navy inspector commands workers to cut the door with a welding torch, Madge tries to entrap Jones by crying rape.

Ironically Bob Jones, a middle-class intellectual, has been trapped by American culture as powerfully as the uneducated Bigger Thomas was in *Native Son*.[7] In both novels, the configurations of race, class, caste, and gender conspire to render the protagonists in postures of guilt. Beaten unconscious and sent to an infirmary, Jones escapes, only to be caught again. Abandoned by Alice, he is brought before a magistrate who, in order to avoid a potential race riot once Madge's flimsy evidence is revealed, consigns Jones to the army, along with two Mexican youths. American justice, and the people behind it, leads Jones to a recognition of his inexorable "guilt" within such a system: "The whole structure of American thought was against me; American tradition had convicted me a hundred years before" (229). Unlike Bigger, however, Bob Jones has sufficient strength to mutter through his bruised lips, "I'm still here" (249). In a sense, the nightmare will continue, but Bob Jones had awakened fully to the relentless ebb and flow of his racial destiny.

The Absurd Vision

The absurd element in *If He Hollers Let Him Go* distinguishes Himes's novel from the more conventional protest fiction of the 1930s and 1940s. While registering his own form of social protest as strongly as Richard Wright, John Steinbeck, John Dos Passos, and Ann Petry, Himes elucidates his cultural concerns within the framework of a grotesque series of sleeping and waking nightmares that undercut both the American dream and the related dream of California as a sort of promised land.

Bob Jones, the archetypically absurd antihero in his fast-moving car, came to California to start a new life. As he moves desperately from episode to episode, his anger and fear are objectified by his sense of the absurd. Indeed, Jones is not a humorless victim in the tradition of Bigger Thomas; he possesses a comic vitality (notably in his nightmares) and a comic perception of his condition that permits him to subdue partially the demonic forces conspiring to subjugate him. Roger Rosenblatt observes perceptively that Jones is "a remarkably funny, quick-witted man, with an expansive and ironic comic imagination."[8] If he is "crazy," then it is the craziness of the Fool in *King Lear*, who perceives the grotesque anarchy of the universe and tries to objectify it through humor.

Filtered through Jones's hard-boiled comic imagination, all people seem to be portrayed in absurd one-dimensional postures. This is not a naturalistic or realistic style but rather the style of the grotesque. Madge, for instance, is a common type, caricatured in absurdist brush strokes: "She was a peroxide blonde with a large-featured, overly-made up face, and she had a large, bright-painted fleshy mouth, kidney-shaped, thinner in the middle than at the ends. Her big blue babyish eyes were mascaraed like a burlesque queen's and there were tiny wrinkles in their corners and about the flare of her nostrils, calipering down about the edges of her mouth" (22). Similarly, Alice is parodied as an Alice-in-Wonderland-type of black woman, while Mr. and Mrs. Harrison babble accommodationist nonsense.

The strength and originality of *If He Hollers Let Him Go* lie in Himes's ability to show how dreams and absurd realities collide in California. Jones, with his high-speed dreams, is one of the most graphic symbols of displaced victims in the fiction of the period. Appropriately Jones embraces his dream most fervently at a southern California drive-in where he proposes to Alice. For a transient moment, they cross "over the river Jordan into the promised land" (207). Himes is ingenious here, and indeed throughout the rest of the novel, in capturing the deceptive sense of freedom engendered by southern California's highway culture. Ironically, the Cook's tour of California that Bob Jones embarks on in five brief days ends for him in a tour of duty. He seems destined to continue his absurd, futile quest, for after the war, the roads of America, filled with racial incongruities, will still await him.

Lonely Crusade

Chester Himes left Los Angeles in 1944 and, receiving a Rosenwald Fellowship, went to New York to await the publication of *If He Hollers Let Him Go*. Quickly losing himself in drunkenness and a series of affairs, he was "shocked back to normalcy" (*The Quality of Hurt*, 76–77) by his wife's attempted suicide and the publication of his first novel. Embittered by the failure of Doubleday to market the novel vigorously or award it Doran's George Washington Carver Memorial Award of $2,500, Himes and Jean in 1945 went to live on her brother Hugo's ranch near Susanville in northern California. Here he wrote the first draft of his second novel, *Lonely Crusade*.

Like his first novel, *Lonely Crusade* is the semiautobiographical product of Himes's California experience. Writing to John Williams, he comments fully on this connection:

Langston has given me a list of people to see—Loren Miller, of course—and a chap named Welford Wilson who had a great influence on my life (inadvertently). Willy Wilson wanted to be a writer: but Willy was a hard-working, conscientious, obedient communist. Willy was working then with the U.S. employment agency by day and with the communists by night. Willy introduced me to all of the important communists (both black and white) in L.A. and I suppose he was assigned to recruit me. Anyway, I was given the works—taken to cell meetings all over town: to parties: to lectures and all that crap. I met all the local heroes of the Spanish Civil War and all the communist script writers—Dalton Trumbo and John Howard Lawson, etc. They housed me and fed me and interviewed me. From lack of work I used to go around with a Negro chap who used to collect salvage from the Hollywood sympathizers to sell for money to be sent to a Spanish refugee camp in Mexico. Most of the brothers in the party used to clothe themselves from the salvage from the Hollywood bigshots—I had more expensive clothes than I've ever had since. But the communists had a use for me. I was used to prove a point. So they would send me out practically every day to apply for work in various firms which did not employ Negroes. I must say here that Los Angeles at that time was as jim crowed as Atlanta, Georgia. The only employment for Negroes was in the kitchen and all white restaurants, bars and many white film theatres refused to serve Negroes. *This is when and where characters in* LONELY CRUSADE *existed and were the same in real life as they were in the book: and a great deal of the narrative and many of the scenes were taken from real life. That is the real reason the communist party hated the book—every character was identifiable—and of course I was Lee Gordon.*[9]

Lonely Crusade, released by Himes's new publisher, Knopf, in 1947, offers in its protagonist, Lee Gordon, a more profound and politically conscious avatar of Bob Jones. Gordon, another of Himes's well-educated middle-class intellectuals, is hired as a union organizer at Comstock Aircraft Corporation in Los Angeles. It is spring 1943, and southern California is once again on parade, the testing ground of Gordon's beliefs.

A long novel of thirty-two chapters, *Lonely Crusade* is the most comprehensive treatment in American fiction of the conflict among blacks, the unions, and the Communist party during World War II. It is a significant political novel in its own right. Unlike Dos Passos, Wright (who had joined the Communist party in 1934), Theodore Dreiser, and others, Himes never seemed seriously beguiled by Marxism, even as he wrote fiction and essays in the 1940s that were exceedingly radical for their day.[10] Lee Gordon's quest for an authentic identity is cast in several dimensions—economic, racial, sexual, existential—but it is ultimately his political identity that gives him unique substance as a character and *Lonely Crusade* its special force as a novel of ideas.

Lee Gordon, born in 1912 in Pasadena to parents who were domestic servants, is a product of the Golden Land. Although a native Californian, he cannot readily embrace the state's vision of limitless possibility. In the eighth grade, he is caught spying on white girls in the school gym and expelled, forcing his parents to leave for Los Angeles. There, shortly after he graduates from high school, his father is killed by Los Angeles police in a case of mistaken identity. By the time he enters UCLA, where he majors in sociology, Gordon is cut off from blacks and whites. For Lee, California is not so much the promised land as a charged territory in which personal and political battles must be fought.

For Gordon, the story of the California is a mythological quest for a world elsewhere. Yet as he drives to work on his first day with the white union organizer Smitty, his promised new beginning is enshrouded in a ghostly landscape: "At Washington Boulevard they turned west, taking their position in the long line of warworkers' cars. Headlights glowed yellow in the gray gloom, and from the flanking murk a drab panorama of one-storied, stuccoed buildings unfolded in monotonous repetition."[11] Similarly, Comstock Aircraft resembles a "huge, flat, sprawling assembly of camouflaged buildings" (17) looming out of the mist. The figurative impact of this landscape is not lost on Gordon, who essentially must read through multiple camouflages and misleading significations in order to decipher the political landscape that he now inhabits. *Lonely Crusade* is about historical and political realities, all too often obscured by an elegiac fondness for the West, and the struggle of one man to create an authentic social and political existence for himself.

Political Existence

The great and complex subject that engages Himes in *Lonely Crusade* is the nature of social and political existence in World War II America. Himes engages assiduously in a critique of this political universe, using his protagonist to debate the conflicts of capitalism and communism, totalitarianism and democracy, the proletariat and the ruling elite, race, religion, and sexuality. Within this matrix of conflicting forces, Gordon must detect and embrace those signs that will give substance to his life.

At the outset of the novel, the prospects for Gordon are not encouraging. At the domestic level defining his personal life, he is alienated from Ruth, his wife of eight years. His relationship with her is sadomasochistic, an enactment of fantasies of power and subjugation that are clearly denied him in the larger world. The acts and language of violence, notably sexual violence, defining his relationship with Ruth, who is a somewhat disembodied figuration of the "good wife," make Gordon an inauthentic personality at a primary dimension of his being. Thus he acts out the paradox, all too common in contemporary American politics, of the would-be crusader whose personal life is profoundly compromised.

Gordon is also alienated from the Comstock workers. He had been hired to organize the 3,000 black men and women who are part of the 30,000-member work force employed at Comstock. However, he is both intimidated by the "sea of white faces" (4) surrounding him and repelled by 95 percent of the black workers, many of them migrants from the South, who are "strangers to him" (62). This "crusader" discovers quickly that he knows nothing about American blacks, even as his own extreme "consciousness of race" (20) menaces and paralyzes his will to act.

If sex and race confound his political existence, the equally intense and subtle conflicts between the labor union and the Communist party also force Gordon to discover and discriminate among the contradictions in his political life. He tends to regard the union leadership warily, seeking signs of commitment. Smitty, a nuts-and-bolts organizer, ultimately becomes his friend. Joe Ptak, a tough national leader who merely "wants to get this plant organized and get the hell out of this screwy town" (261), becomes a sign for the sort of militant courage that eludes Gordon until the end of the novel. Marvin Todd, a racist who is the chairman of the union local, signifies for Gordon the possibility that the union could also become the essential enemy.

Gordon's basic political consciousness, which of necessity must be a radical conscience, is attractive to the American Communist party; however, he is no friend of the party or a fellow traveler. When in the late 1930s he had joined a local Communist organization while working for the postal service, he had learned quickly that the American Communist party would not support resistance to the systematic racism in the civil service. After Pearl Harbor, Lee is suspended by a racist superintendent, but the Communists have conveniently disbanded. Only Executive Order 8802, Roosevelt's directive for fair employment, and the scarcity of labor in 1942 and 1943, return Gordon to the proletariat as a labor organizer.

The debasement of black political consciousness by the American Communist party is symbolized in the incongruous, apelike form of Luther McGregor. Gordon quickly perceives that although Luther belongs to the union, he is also a member of the Communist party. Luther is a case study of the grotesque:

Fully as tall as me, his six-foot height was lost in the thickness of his torso and the width of muscular shoulders that sloped like an ape's, from which hung arms a good foot longer than the average man's. His weird, long-fingered hands of enormous size and grotesque shape, decked with several rings, hung placidly at his side, and his flat, splayed feet seemed comfortably planted in the mud. He wore a belted, light-tan, camel's hair overcoat over a white, turtle-neck sweater, above which his flat-featured, African face seemed blacker than the usual connotation of the word. On his left cheek a puffed bluish scar, with ridges pronging off from it in spokes, was a memento of a pickax duel on a Southern chain gang; and the man who gave him the razor welt, obliquely parting his kinky hair, he always said was dead. (28)

Luther is grotesque because he has been dehumanized by political culture. He will undercut both the union and the Communist party and also take money from the executive vice-president at Comstock, Louis Foster. He has no political loyalties except, in a bizarre way, to Lee Gordon.

One of Himes's prime motives in *Lonely Crusade* is to expose the Marxist mythology in the United States. To this end, he develops scenes and episodes throughout the novel that amount to a polemic against the American Communist party. Essentially he indicts the party because it is not genuinely interested in proletarian revolution or in the lives of American blacks. Its revolutionary rhetoric merely masks petit-bourgeois pretensions and aspirations. A Communist cocktail party riddled with incongruities becomes an emblem of the debased political consciousness of Communist proselytizers. Luther's consort, Mollie, a white woman, is no more or less grotesque than other intellectual revelers: "In the green light her hair was bright orange and her skin an embalmed white" (78). Other partygoers spout Marx and extol Stalin with hyperboles that Lee himself deflates, for Gordon has a talent for dissecting Communists. The cult of Marx is simply another misleading sign for Gordon: "Now everyone was drunk. Many had reverted to what they had been before they had become Communists" (97). Lee understands his political situation. He refuses to be an inert victim or political tool. Nevertheless, he renders himself vulnerable to manipulation because of fundamental weaknesses in his sexual identity, a weakness masking greater personal and social evasions.

Sexual Existence

The predatory nature of Gordon's behavior toward his wife, Ruth, manifests itself as rape. This violence is reflected obversely in his relationship with Jackie Forks, a white woman whom he meets at the party and who is a Communist assigned by the party to compromise him sexually. Given her duplicitous nature, Lee's liaison with Jackie at base is a fabrication of social reality or an evasion of it. He suspects that Jackie is a Communist plant but strives through sex with her to destroy the barriers separating black and white existence. In the end, both become alienated players in a game that neither can win.

As Gordon careens between Ruth and Jackie, he becomes an accomplice in a conspiracy of evasion designed to alienate him from his political task. Gordon's "loneliness" is articulated through this frenetic struggle to achieve sexual communion with Jackie, an impossibility for two people immersed in racist culture. Essentially there is never an equal emotional or sexual partnership between Gordon and Jackie; rather their passion becomes an amplification of their separateness. At one point in chapter 24, they sit in a café on Western Avenue listening to Nat King Cole's "I'm Lost," a sign or prefiguration of their relationship. Neither can achieve liberation through the other.

To liberate oneself authentically requires the ability to free one's existence from all mythologies of sexual power. This Lee is unable to do, and it cripples his will. For Jackie, her inability to transcend a sexual fascination for a black man, her fear of being caught in "a Negro emotional mess" (301) as the other woman, and her mission with the Communist party undermine any possibility of a valid relationship. With considerable patience and skill, Himes unmasks the ways in which a corrupt misapplication of sexual desires destructively exploits people socially, economically, and politically.

Himes posits in *If He Hollers Let Him Go* and *Lonely Crusade* the thesis that sexual crises both precipitate and reflect social and political conflicts. In *Lonely Crusade* he moves more persistently into those structures of distorted sexual feeling that manifest equally political deformations. Both Jackie and Lee—like Luther and Mollie—permit themselves to be forced into a sexual battleground. They never discover appropriate gestures or vocabulary to validate their relationship. In fact, both are personally and politically compromised by it. Gordon's reputation as a union leader is blemished when the Communists betray Jackie and set her up as a union informer. Jackie, in turn, succumbing to race hatred, turns Lee in as an accomplice in the death of a corrupt sheriff's deputy in the employ of the Comstock president, whom Luther has killed. Lee Gordon is trapped in a predatory process of sexual and political attrition that has a sterilizing effect on his existence.

Authentic Existence

Against the predatory forces in his life, Lee Gordon must seek varieties of commitment that might validate his existence. He does not seem to be temperamentally or historically equipped for his crusader's role; he has trouble mobilizing his inner resources as well as the workers. Nevertheless, he does attain a measure of authenticity by refusing to embrace individuals who are avatars of what he could become and by aligning himself in the end with a guru of sorts.

Luther McKinley is one grotesque avatar—a premonition of what Lee's behavior is pushing him toward. His violence—notably as he rises "like a great black monster" (318) to kill the sheriff's deputy, Paul Dixon—fails to achieve anything, however, because it cannot destroy the universal reality of oppressive culture. Crazed and yet astute, Luther perceives his "niggerness" and conveys a lesson in historicism to Gordon: "In this goddamned world, they's all kind of wars going on and people is getting kilt in all of them. They's the races fighting 'gainst each other. And they's the classes cutting each other's throats. And they's every mother's son fighting for hisself, just to keep on living. And they's the nigger at the bottom of it all, being fit by everybody—the white folks and the black folks, the capitalists and the Communists, too" (327). Amoral and uncommitted, Luther is ultimately killed while resisting arrest.

A second even more deracinated doppelgänger is Lester McKinley, a well-educated former schoolteacher who works at Comstock and wants to kill Louis Foster. McKinley suffers from a homicidal mania induced by racial oppression. Married to a white woman, Sylvia, and living with her and their children in what superficially resembles interracial bliss, McKinley knows that racism has made him mentally ill. He declares to Lee, "I strive for sanity more than intelligence" (75). Controlled by the system, an imminent reflection of Lee's possible fate, McKinley disappears from the novel before he can enact his fantasies and kill Foster.

Louis Foster is not so much an avatar for Lee as he is an invitation to comfortable middle-class existence in American society. The symbol of craven opportunism and elitism in a reactionary world, Foster invites Lee and Ruth to his Pasadena estate, where he offers Lee a $5,000 annual salary in the personnel department if he leaves his union organizer's position: "Foster could not bear to have a Negro, any Negro, dislike him. And before he would allow a Negro to really hate him, he would make the Negro rich" (181). For Lee, lunch with Foster is a grueling rehearsal of the dialectics of power in capitalist society. Rather than succumb to Foster's irredeemable worldview, Gordon politely declines the offer. While Himes leaves unresolved the question of Gordon's ultimate identity, we sense a combative humanism in him that might authenticate his existence.

Virtually every significant character in Gordon's universe forces him to redefine himself in terms of the conflict between humanism and antihumanism. The most positive humanistic relationship elaborated in the novel is that between Lee and Abe Rosenberg, an older member of the Communist party and the keenest intellectual in the group. Rosenberg believes in a humanistic Marxism, and his droll, down-to-earth demeanor tests Gordon at all times. For one thing, Lee must overcome a penchant for Semitic stereotyping: "Sitting on a disbanded wooden casing, feet dangling and his froglike body wrapped in a wrinkled tan cotton slack suit, Rosie looked the picture of the historic Semite" (151). Through long dialogues with Rosie, Lee begins to understand clearly the ramifications of power and powerlessness throughout history. First he must purge himself of anti-Semitism, acknowledging Rosenberg's statement, "Of all the rotten results of racial prejudice . . . anti-Semitism in the Negro is the worst" (152). A spiritual guide for Gordon and one of the sharpest, most sympathetic characters in all of Himes's fiction, the older Rosenberg teaches his protégé the "habits of survival" (160) that must link all oppressed people in every form of society.

Through a continuing series of dialogues with Abe Rosenberg that help to structure the novel, Lee Gordon moves from a posture of passivity and wavering commitment to one of authentic commitment. In the last six days framing the conclusion of the novel, Gordon works assiduously but apparently without success to get out the black vote for the union. Rosie, who has been drummed out of the Communist party for his contrary support of Lee and his denunciation of Luther, provides Lee with the progressive, humanistic rationale that ultimately energizes him: "People are important not because of what they do but because of what they are. The fact of being people is important. Therefore it holds that being Negroes who are people is indivisibly important. People may be divided and races may be divided, but the fact of their existence and the importance of the fact, are indivisible" (376). Lee himself comes to a similar existential recognition "that he could not excuse his predicament on grounds of race. This time he alone was to blame—Lee Gordon, a human being, one of the cheap, weak people of the world" (361). With this self-revelation, Lee is prepared to accept Rosie's dictum that "all is progressive movement" (578) and the imminent possibility of his death as a crusader, for Rosie's final function in the novel is to prepare Lee for affirmation through death.

Some critics find Lee's shift from reaction to action too sudden.[12] It is more appropriate to assert that Gordon, as a thinking being, has been attempting to comprehend his behavior through the fifty days of narrative constituting *Lonely Crusade* and that, with Abe Rosenberg's help (and also Smitty's allegiance), he is now prepared to act. The conversion of Meursault in Camus's *The Stranger* to a posture of existential rebellion is also abrupt but based on an unfolding recognition of the oppressive essence of his condition. Like Meursault, Lee Gordon seizes his existence and embraces the gestures and actions of rebellion on the day of the union rally.

We sense in the penultimate confrontation between the workers and the police at the end of *Lonely Crusade* the conjunction of many of the power drives throughout American history. Hunted by the police for his role in the Dixon murder, Lee nevertheless abandons his cover in a union sound truck and races to pick up the union banner from the fallen Joe Ptak. He reaches Ptak, snatches the union flag, and begins marching down the street as a deputy sheriff's gun begins to draw a bead on his life: "It was as if this was the moment he had lived for—not the choice of a conclusion, nor the facing of a fact, but this was the knowledge of a truth" (397).

In the melodramatically staged conclusion of *Lonely Crusade*, Himes wants us to understand that the cost of Lee Gordon's ethical and political rebellion is death. This affirmation of one's fate through death is the judgment inherent not only in existential philosophy but in classical tragedy. Gordon finally comprehends the signs of his culture and the need to rebel. Rosie once acknowledged, "You may die for the murder of Paul Dixon. But once you resolve your indecision toward life and embrace your own reality, you will not be afraid to die" (397). In refusing to accept this dehumanization and in embracing a progressive ideology, Lee Gordon acts—becomes a crusader—with the knowledge that his death can have meaning in an absurdly oppressive world.

The absurd world—Los Angeles during the war years—has demanded from Lee Gordon a recognition of the need for a new sense of reality. Early in the novel, he had perceived with photographic clarity the nature of this world: "Niggers alongside nigger-haters. Jews bucking rivets for Jew-baiters. Native daughters lunching with Orientals. Lumped together in war plants. Soldiers on the home-front now. For this was a war-production city. The birthplace of the P-48. Womb of the Liberty Ship. Weak end of the armed forces. The bloated, hysterical, frantic, rushing city that was Los Angeles in the spring of 1943" (130). In this new American crucible, Lee Gordon has a "sickening sense of being crazy in a crazy world—an idiot among idiots, all speaking an unknown tongue" (141). From his awareness of this absurd world and a recognition of his inadequacies, Gordon forges a new self—an activist self empowered to crusade against the absurdities of class culture.

Suppression

While ostensibly a protest novel, *Lonely Crusade* is more broadly an eloquent subtext on American culture's obsession with domination and power. Cerebral, problematic, original in content, the novel is a difficult one for the critic seeking to gain access to it. It is an intricate text about a specific cultural moment. As a moral treatise on the temptations to power and the varieties of political control, it demands an astute audience. *Lonely Crusade* puzzled many reviewers and angered several constituencies when it was published in 1947. Great in scope and ambition—one of the most radical novels about the structures of American domination and about California life as a symptom of the corrupt power of both capitalism and communism—*Lonely Crusade* was reviled by critics of both the left and the right.

On the day of publication, 8 October 1947, Himes discovered that most of the interviews, appearances, and book signings that had previously been arranged for him had been cancelled abruptly. These included scheduled appearances on the Mary McBride radio program and a CBS program, as well as appearances at Macy's and Bloomingdale's. Himes suspected Communist intimidation, which was reinforced by vitriolic reviews in *New Masses*, the *Daily Worker*, and *People's Voice*. Yet criticism ran the ideological spectrum. *Atlantic Monthly* declared, "Hate runs through this book like a streak of yellow bile," while *Commentary* compared it to "graffiti on the walls of public toilets."[15]

In *The Quality of Hurt*, Himes declares that he has tried to write fairly "of the fear that inhabits the minds of all blacks who live in America, and the various impacts on this fear precipitated by Communism, industrialism, Unionism, the war, white women, and marriage within the race" (101). Refusing to subscribe to any ideology, Himes in *Lonely Crusade* gives dramatic embodiment to the interlocking structures of oppression in American life. The novel is rich in the dynamic relationships of people to their historical and cultural situation, but whites and blacks, the left and the right, Jews and Christians, did not like Himes's critique. America was in an ideological shift away from Himes, and he was swimming against the current. In effect, the impulse of critics was to suppress the novel. Stung by this assault, Himes lapsed into a five-year period when he found it difficult to write. And the hostile reception of *Lonely Crusade* convinced him to leave the United States forever if he had the chance.

Chapter Three
Strange Landscape: *Cast the First Stone*

Following the savage attacks on *Lonely Crusade*, Chester Himes experienced a prolonged period of devitalization as a writer. In *The Quality of Hurt*, he admits, "For the next five years I couldn't write. I reworked my prison novel, *Black Sheep*, cutting it down to half its original size, and I tried to write a stage play from *If He Hollers Let Him Go*, but those were just reflex motions" (103). His agent at the time was Margot Johnson, who had sold the motion picture rights to Willard Motley's prison novel, *Knock on Any Door*, for $65,000, but she could not place *Black Sheep*. Himes had changed the novel's title over the years, from *Day after Day* (1936) to *The Way It Was* (1939), to *Black Sheep*, moving from first-person to third-person narratives to first and back. Finally, Johnson sold the novel to Coward-McCann for a $1,200 advance—money that ultimately would enable Himes to make his passage to France in 1953.

Between the publication of *Lonely Crusade* in 1947 and the release of *Cast the First Stone* in 1952, Himes spent time at Yaddo, the writers' colony in Saratoga Springs, New York, but more typically he moved from job to job, serving variously as a caretaker, porter, or bellhop at estates and hotels in the New York metropolitan area. In the summer of 1948, Himes delivered an address, "The Dilemma of the Negro Novelist in the United States," at the University of Chicago. This document captures both his personal anguish as a creative writer during the period and his persistently radical posture as an artist. A critique of the cultural condition, "The Dilemma of the Negro Artist in the United States" offers a succinct and remarkably graphic historical vision of the impact of oppression on the black American writer.

At the outset, Himes asserts that the black writer "must discover from his experiences the truth of his oppressed existence in terms that will provide some meaning to his life."[1] Beset by personal, environmental, and artistic constraints, the black writer must acknowledge that he or she has inherited the moral burden of racial history. This black writer, to remain true, must embark on "an intellectual crusade that will take him through the horrors of the damned" (53). Revealing a national corruption rooted in racism and a progressive degeneration of black life caused by this historical reality will al-

ienate the black writer from both white and black readers. These, nevertheless, "are the daily horrors, the daily realities, the daily experiences of an oppressed minority" (57). Publishers are not particularly interested in black
writers who chronicle "centuries of oppression." Thus the black writer must
devise strategies to reveal rather than hide "his beaten, battered soul, his
dwarfed personality, his scars of oppression" (55).

To get his prison novel published, Himes himself had to engage in subterfuge. Nevertheless, an essential question that Himes asks in his essay echoes
in *Cast the First Stone*: "Can you abuse, enslave, persecute, segregate and gen-
erally oppress a people, and have them love you for it?" (156). Even in changing the masks of the characters in his prison novel, Himes in *Cast the First
Stone* probes the indomitable universal quality of the human spirit to resist
oppression and brutalization—to find ways to transcend the perversities and
absurdities of a degenerate culture.

The Novel as Confessional

By the time that Himes was paroled from Ohio State Penitentiary in 1936
after serving seven and a half years of his twenty-year sentence, he had come
to his vocation as a writer. Much of *Black Sheep*, told from the third-person
point of view of a white prisoner whose life mirrored that of Himes, had been
completed. Moreover, Himes had written several prison stories—notably
"Crazy in the Stir," "To What Red Hell," "The Visiting Hour," "The Night's
For Cryin'" and "Every Opportunity," all published in *Esquire* between 1934
and 1937—which became part of the terrain depicted ultimately in *Cast the
First Stone*.[2]

Himes's task in the early short fiction and the expanded and reconstituted
final product, *Cast the First Stone*, is to account for the oppressive forms of
experience that coalesce within the prison system of America. For Himes,
prison life offers a symbiotic system—people, objects, structures—defining
the lives of individuals who have become socially marginal figures in the
American landscape. Himes elaborated this connection in a 1952 letter to
Richard Wright: "This book is a simple story about life in prison; maybe the
boys can stand the truth about life in a state prison better than they can stand
the truth about life in the prison of being a Negro in America."[3] As Himes's
first-person protagonist and persona in the novel, James Monroe, comes to
understand, the mind must fashion an understanding of those signs generated by the prison world if it is to envision and achieve any form of liberation.

Himes indicated at the beginning of his autobiography that he could not
remember much of his prison experience, and indeed he seems reticent in *The*

Quality of Hurt to discuss it; he engages in a deliberate psychological and linguistic effort to forget. Yet in *Cast the First Stone*, through his first-person
persona, Himes did find the language to "confess" (a word that echoes
through the novel from the first chapter) to his chilling encounter with prison
life. In 1947 Himes wrote to Van Vechten on the liberating effect of *Cast the
First Stone*: "As I look back now I find much of my retardation as a writer has
been due to a subconscious (and conscious and deliberate) desire to escape
my past."[4] The fundamental act that Jim Monroe (Chester Himes) engages
in is existential recitation, meditation, confession. Renamed prisoner number
109130, he must find a more authentic identity for himself than a series of
integers or risk not just marginality and entrapment but ultimate
destruction.

Jim Monroe, a nineteen-year-old prisoner sentenced to twenty to twenty-
five years for armed robbery, is clearly an avatar of Himes. For Himes, this
autobiographical novel helps him to recreate a self and to restore through fiction a painful period in his life. The literal act of confessing to those existential ruptures begins in the first chapter of *Cast the First Stone* where, in a
scene paralleling Himes's own experience, Monroe remembers the confession
beaten out of him by the Chicago police:

> I could feel the cops hitting me in the mouth, hanging me by my handcuffed feet up-
> side down over a door, beating my legs with their gun butts. I could feel the blood
> running down my legs from where the handcuffs pinched them on the ankle-bone.
> I had stood it as long as I could, I thought, looking at the ceiling. I might have
> stood it longer if I'd lost consciousness. But there had been too much pain and not
> enough hurt to lose consciousness. I had confessed.[5]

In "confessing" the protagonist passes paradoxically from one estranged community to another. However, in the closed world of prison life, Monroe's task
is to find a new name—a new identity—for himself, as well as a place in his
new community. What he confesses to in telling his tale of prison life is nothing less than his dangerous passage through a potentially annihilative American institution to eventual freedom.

A Strange World

James Monroe's initial entrance into prison is both a constricting and a bizarre experience: "It was my first night in the dormitory. It was strange.
Everything was strange" (3). This sense of strangeness will come full circle at
the end of the novel when, leaving prison six years later, the hero declares, "It

felt strange to be outside" (346). Yet within the boundaries of his new prison community, Monroe must come to full consciousness of the strangeness of his environment—the grotesqueness of his condition—if he is to mediate successfully or map his way through dangers of his closed, claustrophobic world.

The world that Monroe enters is an absurd imitation of outside culture. Inside the prison walls he discovers that many primal referents—sexual, racial, social, political, economic—encountered in the outside culture take on involuted institutional forms. Cultural referents abound: the church, the school, the workplace, the dormitory, the playing field. A primitive form of barter capitalism, tolerated and abetted by the prison hierarchy, is the dominant economic system; the prison itself is a crude vehicle for mass production. The prison's political structure is animated by the pure application of power from the warden to his deputies to the guards. The prisoners themselves play power games, but within shifting patterns of class, caste, and race they manage to establish and sustain a paradoxically viable community, or "club." H. Bruce Franklin, in a trenchant analysis of *Cast the First Stone*, correctly places the bizarre culture of Himes's prison novel at the center of his fictional universe: "The contradictions Himes expresses about his prison life cannot be resolved. Indeed, these contradictions are the very life of his fiction, with all its seething tension, appalling violence, macabre comedy, bizarre shifts in plot, and agony relieved only by occasional bursts of some future apocalyptic redemption."[6] Thus within the physical and normative limitations of the prison environment, there are numerous signs of American absurdity triggered by social and political control.

Young Monroe, sandwiched among 4,000 convicts in a prison designed for 1,800, must deal with the problematics of his condition. Although his prison world is "strange" in the sense that it represents a discontinuity from life outside the prison's walls and disruptions of one form or the other inside these walls, Monroe instantly begins to perceive a formal social dynamics at work. For instance, he is initially assigned to a coal detail, a job previously handled by black convicts but now delegated to whites as special punishment. Moreover, from his first entrance into the prison dormitory, he is sized up by veteran convicts in largely sexual or homoerotic terms. One convict, Mal Streator, who has learned how to manipulate the prison system, serves as Jim's mentor and protector, sublimating his own homoerotic impulses by convincing Monroe that they should pretend they are cousins. Another of Monroe's early experiences centers on the violence of prison life as a new prisoner, Jackson, beats up a guard. The convicts are jubilant: "Everybody was talking and laughing and excited, as if they were at a ball game and seen one of their home team hit a home run" (33). From these three episodes, Monroe perceives problems of race, gender, and class as they are reflected in curiously involuted forms within the power structures of prison life.

Although Himes felt induced to change the racial identity of his protagonist and, apparently, many other key characters—a strange act of aesthetic involution or sublimation in its own right—he nevertheless succeeds in demonstrating the ways in which the ideology of a minority culture can remain intact within an oppressive system. The prison convicts, a composite of black and white humanity, are a minority culture who must reconstruct a community for themselves under trying conditions. Each person carries the mark—his prison number—of difference from the majority culture. The outside culture would reduce these minority figures to anonymity quite literally by unnaming them, by giving them prisoner numbers. Thus Himes's task is to transform these minority figures in a regimented penal system into a mirror of American culture. In a paradoxical way, he must continue, as he did in his first two published novels, to write minority literature, a literature that illuminates a "strange" universe for readers in the American mainstream.

Himes was in an ideal position to make readers see how the strange world of minority culture informs the total culture of the United States. In this connection, Walter J. Ong offers a compelling reason for studying a text such as *Cast the First Stone* in terms of those ideological perspectives activated by minority literature: "A minority literature often mixes what is unfamiliar to the majority culture with what is familiar. It thus provides not only an organization of experience different from that of the majority culture (and of other minorities) but also an interactive organization. A minority literature often negotiates for its own identity with the majority culture and constantly redefines itself, ultimately bringing the majority culture to define itself more adequately, too."[7] For Chester Himes, the American prison becomes a prime artifact mediating between majority and minority culture, an explanatory device to articulate an unknown community for the white establishment.

Seen as a work offering a critique of the one institutional form of American oppression that reduces all humanity to minority status, *Cast the First Stone* contains the same tendencies that inform Himes's first two published novels. Earlier critics overlook this continuity in Himes's evolving vision of capitalist society on the verge of discord and chaos. Stephen Milliken, for example, states that Himes in *Cast the First Stone* "eliminated the entire subject of racism, the central theme of his first two novels."[8] James Lundquist similarly suggests that in moving away from the racially charged *If He Hollers Let Him Go* and *Lonely Crusade*, Himes creates "assimilationist" or "integrationist" fiction.[9] In fact, there is a galaxy of secondary black convicts in the novel who remind readers that race and racism are part of the American dilemma in virtually every phase of social and institutional life. Moreover, all prisoners, black and white, became part of the constitutive metaphor of the prison as the human dumping ground of capitalist culture. As H. Bruce Franklin asserts, "Literature about crime and criminals is central to bourgeois culture."[10] Himes's novel, while refusing to sentimentalize a convict population capable of heinousness and depravity, serves ultimately to expose the larger tyranny and arbitrary oppression of a system that seems unrestrained by its own penchant for law and order. As for the convict-narrator who exposes this system, Jimmy Monroe is the "deviant," the outsider, the alien, the minority figure who must learn how to resist the tyranny of his condition.

The Convict as Rebel

Although Himes populates his prison novel with thieves, rapists, forgers, murderers, pederasts, and con artists—the conventional picaresques of criminal fiction—his far more ambitious objective is to expose the criminality of the prison system itself. All of the convicts stand in opposition to their culture by virtue of their crimes and their degrading and dehumanizing incarceration. Monroe's own harsh sentence, reflecting the excessive verdict rendered the nineteen-year-old Himes, is a preliminary indictment of the legal system. As first-person narrator, his task is thus not only confessional but ideological: he must accept responsibility for his crime but also find a more intricate language to reveal the institutional usurpation of justice in America whereby the punishment does not fit the crime. Beneath the hard-boiled surface realism of the narrator's style, readers must listen carefully for the language of subversion that permits James Monroe to become not a conventional criminal but a political prisoner who rebels against the imposition of unbridled and arbitrary power.

From the beginning, Monroe has a sensory and cognitive apprehension of the coordinates of his new world. He has been placed within a framework that denies human liberation. This is an alien environment in space and time, defined by the harsh geometry of walls. At the end of his first day in prison, Monroe experiences a cold, hushed landscape that makes coherent the nature of his closed world:

I turned my head and looked out the window that was just a little above the level of my eyes. I saw the moon in a deep blue sky and a guard-turret with spotlights down the walls. I saw the guard silhouetted against the sky, a rifle cradled in his arm, the intermittent glow of the cigarette in his mouth. I saw the long black sweep of the walls beneath the deep blue distance. When you looked at the walls your vision stopped. Everything stopped at the walls. The walls were about fifty feet from the dormitory building. Just fifty feet away was freedom, I thought. Fifty feet—and twenty years. (18)

Everything, as Himes intimates in one translucent sentence, stops at the walls: space is constricted; linear history regresses or becomes repetitive; human behavior goes neither backward nor forward. Nevertheless, to see and remember the contours of this world is a primary strategy for resisting the powerful ability of a closed world to obliterate identity.

Monroe is young and intelligent, possessing (like Himes) some college education. He is able to think critically about the dialectics of prison life and the mechanisms of control that such dialectics presume. Despite his youthful innocence, his anxieties and fears, he has the critical ability to remain consciously intractable. While many of the jailers and the jailed demonstrate a diminished or largely effaced political and social consciousness of their condition, the narrator adheres rigorously to the logic of resistance and rebellion. For instance, in chapter 4, Monroe refuses on principle to work when shifted from the porter detail back to the coal brigade. Classified as totally disabled because of an accident before he was committed to prison, he rejects forced labor, an act of defiance that results in a night in a correction cell—the hole. The next day he does go to work as a teacher but is demoted to pupil for failing to define a predicate adjective. Monroe learns quickly that resistance can assume many guises, that subterfuge is often a more successful ploy than physical rebelliousness. Subsequently he learns to move through a variety of easy jobs or to avoid work altogether, trading on a "disability" now validated by prison authorities.

Just as he learns to defy the prison authorities actively and passively, Monroe also develops a portfolio of talents that empower him within the convict community. From his monthly disability payments, he distributes small favors to the community. With another side of his personality, his temper and impetuousness, he keeps convicts off balance yet grateful for his friendship. Above all, his rapid ascendancy to top poker player conveys celebrity status; with another convict, Blocker, he runs the largest and most lucrative card game in the prison. Even his youthful sexuality is part of his repertoire, for he has a palpably untouched physicality that interests many of the prisoners. His easy ability to strike up friendships and instill loyalty permits him to control his situation by the end of the first year. The convicts "toadied to me. They made up my bunk for me in the morning, shined my shoes, laundered my pyjamas, underwear and socks, pressed my uniform. They considered it a

privilege to talk to me. It all cost me plenty. Everything cost me plenty"
(124–25). By turning a critical gaze on the convict community, Monroe
manages his condition while avoiding the grosser manifestations of violence,
degradation, and dissolution afflicting most of the rest of the prisoner population. Within shifting institutional patterns of oppression, he avoids total
control.

The Self and Others

Unlike the mass of convicts whose fates are as fixed as their prison sentences, Monroe has a capacity for growth. His ability to achieve a metamorphosis of his personality is a prime strategy of resistance, for it assaults the
penitentiary's institutional instinct for stasis—for the rendering of humanity
as faceless prisoners without any will. In fact, in the six years that he is in
prison, the narrator attaches himself to convicts, and these key pairings take
Monroe through various modes of being. Within the social context of *Cast
the First Stone*, Monroe enjoys an amplitude of primary and secondary relationships that induce in him a fluid and evolving consciousness.

Four primary relationships serve to structure large segments of the novel
and also to reveal the metamorphic forms of being that Monroe passes
through. In the early chapters, the relationship between Mal and Jimmy pre-
dominates, a pairing characterized largely by Monroe's dependency on the
somewhat older convict's knowledge of the prison system. They look so
much alike that they pass as "cousins," a ploy that appeals to the elegant
Mal's suppressed homophilia. By the end of the tenth chapter, the relationship has changed, with Mal now dependent on Monroe for occasional loans.

As Mal and Jimmy's relationship lapses, a new pairing develops between
Monroe and a prisoner named Blocker. Together they run the biggest and
most lucrative gambling game in the prison. Blocker, also older than
Monroe, is a "little, humpbacked, sharp-faced fellow" (111) whom Jimmy
immediately likes. From Blocker, Monroe learns to temper his pity for the
rest of the convict population with a more robust skepticism. When they are
running their poker or dice games, he adheres to Blocker's maxim, "Never
give a sucker a break." As entrepreneurs and gambling czars, they are so successful that they hire assistants, franchising the operation in a comic assault
on the prison's own forms of exploitative capitalism. They are "straight
friends," gambling buddies who impose a successful mode of cultural control
on their environment.

Shortly after Monroe's emerging partnership with Blocker, the narrator
encounters Metz, who becomes Jimmy's intellectual companion. Himes of-

fers a graphic portrait of Metz in a grotesque description that is the common mode of the novel: "He had a narrow, rather handsome, very reckless face with curly black hair cut GI fashion, and the arteries stood out in his large-fingered hands, jerking nervously on the table. There was a ragged scar down the middle of his forehead to the bridge of his nose and now, in his hot red face, it was livid like a jagged line of clotted blood; and as I watched it seemed to twitch as if it was a separate living entity from his face" (137). Although he strikes prisoners as a man capable of killing anyone, Metz nurtures the cognitive and aesthetic components of Monroe's personality. The narrator acknowledges this unique connection and its impact on his perception of liberation: "Our companionship was strangely separate from all my other prison activities. Although Blocker and I were still running our poker game and Mal and I were still good cousins, the companionship between Metz and myself did not include either of them, nor the poker game, nor any other phase of prison activity. It was as if we were members of the same club and had discovered a common interest in chess and conversation" (139–40). Together the "professor" and the "kid," as they are labeled, discuss literature, religion, law, and sexuality in prison. Through Metz, the narrator embraces ideas, developing an interest in writing and in correspondence courses in law. No longer philosophically or artistically faceless, Monroe becomes endowed with a new sense of understanding and purpose as he grows, paradoxically, within the confinements of the prison.

One final primary relationship expands the configurations of the narrator's consciousness: the almost redemptive affair between Monroe and a new prisoner, Duke Dido, which begins in chapter 22 and carries through to the end of the novel. Young, vulnerable, injured, and hobbling, Dido is a grotesque incarnation of Monroe when he arrived in prison five years earlier. What distinguishes the two is that Dido is not at all ambivalent about his sexuality. He is homosexual, and in his insolent, often hysterical way, he courts the narrator, "the Jimmy Monroe who writes" (254) and who becomes his protector and companion.

One of the most distinctive features of *Cast the First Stone* is Himes's subtle and scrupulous depiction of male sexuality in prison life, an aspect of the novel that offended or perplexed several reviewers when the book was published.[11] Clearly the painful marginality of the prisoners' lives induces many of them to refashion their heterosexuality, turning it toward what Himes terms boy-girl relationships among men. In fact, there is a special boy–girl company created by prison officials for overtly homosexual prisoners, but all dormitory life seems propelled by the rhythm of homosexuality. Dido, with his ukulele, his "grotesque walk," and his "throat lovely as a woman's" (249), forces Monroe to confront the need for love as he recreates his identity.

Himes implies that a truly new self is incomplete if deprived of both the physicality and erotic power of love. Dido is a mysterious, compelling, tantalizing presence in Monroe's life. There is something bizarre about him: "His shoulders were rather wide but stooped, and in walking his body slouched and all of his movements were awkward and jerky and grotesque. Every step seemed a precarious action, bordering on actual disaster" (248). Dido is the only individual who throws Monroe into a specific sexual context of self-discovery. Although in the final version of the novel he never physically consummates the relationship that Dido yearns for, Monroe feels—and apprehends—a sexual intimacy with the younger man. In earlier manuscript versions of the novel, where the homoerotic tone is much stronger, there is evidence that Monroe has a sexual relationship with his young companion. For example, in the *Yesterday Will Make You Cry* manuscript, Monroe, acknowledging physical intimacy with Rico (the original name for Dido), says, "Even if I am guilty, no guard actually caught me." And Rico intersperses, "*We* sounds better."[12] In fact, Himes had known a Rico or "Prince Rico," a black prisoner from Georgia, while in Ohio Penitentiary. He was in his early twenties when Himes knew him, a singer who collected black working chanteys. Their relationship apparently was close.[13]

While enjoying the "grotesque unreality" (307) of life with Dido and insisting on a sort of platonic homoeroticism, Monroe nevertheless knows that this paradoxical relationship is transcendent in its power. Even as the dorm turns against them and a friendly guard warns the narrator that he is jeopardizing a chance for early parole, Monroe persists in a difficult human affair. Their relationship is an act of defiance—a manifestation of Eros and community—one that literally transforms Jimmy's last months in prison. "Everything touched me that spring" (297), he confesses. The narrator's extended meditation on the creation of authentic selfhood through resistance to normative limitations ends with Dido's suicide, which obliterates their relationship but prepares Jimmy Monroe for his final metamorphosis into a new life beyond prison walls.

Resurrection

Just as a series of segmented relationships propels the protagonist toward a reconstituted identity and ultimate liberation, one heightened and immutable event forces Monroe to confront the primal absurdity and horror of prison life: the Easter fire and riot that Himes presents in chapters 14 through 16.

These chapters serve as the structural and metaphysical center of *Cast the First Stone*. The episode is based historically on the Easter Monday fire that ravaged Ohio State Penitentiary on 21 April 1930, burning 317 convicts to death, prompting Himes's early story, "To What Red Hell."[14]

Himes turns this disastrous event into a theater of the grotesque, a graphic and harrowing meditation on the consequences of centralized institutional power. The fire begins in the 10 and 11 block on Easter Monday evening as Monroe and Metz are "talking bout the fatalism of Omar Khayyam" (143). It spreads quickly to the 7 and 8 block, then to the 5–8 cell house, engulfing enormous chunks of the prison "like a huge, fire-eating monster sucking in the flame and smoke upon the writhing convicts in its belly" (145). Guards, convicts, and prison administrators become crazed figures in a nightmarish Boschean world. They turn into an uncaged, surging mob. Monroe, who prior to the event had been coping poorly with the monotony of his days in prison and the prospect of an interminable prison sentence, is caught in this cycle of grotesque exhilaration and horror:

I started running across the yard with that high-stepping sense of being too tall to stay on the ground, that marijuana gives you. The harder I ran the less distance I covered. I felt as if I was running up and down in the same spot. I ran harder, lifted my feet higher, until I was churning with motion, going nowhere. And then I stepped into something. I looked down and saw that I had stepped into a burnt-up convict's belly and had pushed out huge globules of vomit through his tightly clenched teeth and over his black-burned face. (146)

Alternately fascinated and repelled by this infernal landscape, nauseated by the sights of the dead and the screams of convicts being burned alive in their locked cells, Monroe feels that his consciousness is being shocked into full awareness of the chaos around him.

The fire burns away Monroe's fixed cultural fate as a prisoner. First he feels exposed to death: "Worms began crawling in my stomach. I backed out of the chapel, into the chaotic night, feeling those worms crawling in my stomach as if I, too, was dead and in the ground and already rotting" (151). Next, within the Kafkaesque absurdity of the scene, this "Sodom and Gomorrah in the flower of its vulgarity, stark and putrid and obscene, grotesque and nauseating" (166), Monroe learns the extremes and limitations of his own humanity. He is not a hero, as are many others. Conversely, he does not rob the dead, nor does he engage in "bitchery and abomination," although in one frenzied moment he runs into Mal and propositions him. Finally, within this

crazed metamorphic flow of identity, he sheds himself of the memory—of
the guilt—of his previous criminal existence.

Himes renders the Easter Monday holocaust superbly as a symbolic enactment of prison life as purgatory. Gradually the dehumanizing ideology of the
penitentiary is restored and for a time, a new, fascist order prevails. The most
lethal of the experienced guards, Cody, becomes head lieutenant. He presides
over a new cadre of guards whose names—Pick Handle Slim, Dog Back,
Hangman—are comic clues to their macabre and sadistic purpose. Nevertheless, Monroe wanders in a new landscape, suddenly conscious of his
rights—"furious, boiling with all that hot rebellion I'd been feeling of late
against the least thing that appeared to jeopardize my rights" (177). After the
dead are counted and the damage assessed, changes in the penal code reduce
the narrator's sentence by thirteen and a half years. Still not an exemplary
prisoner, the narrator can interpret his world anew and manage his life in
order to assert his rights.

Monroe emerges from the infernal world bounded by the Easter Monday
fire and its aftermath with a new authorial voice. Redeemed by fire, possessing a growing political consciousness that prompts him to study law and pe-
tition the governor, he seeks an evolving and coherent definition of himself as
a free person, even within the restructured universe of the penitentiary.
Monroe is now possessed by the idea of freedom. Indeed Himes tells a trium-
phant and often comic tale of a hero who must discover "the way to freedom"
(346). In the end, as he walks from the prison walls to be taken to the prison
farm that will be a midpoint on his road to liberation, Monroe is still rebel-
lious, knowing that the hideous and absurd features of the penitentiary have
not destroyed him. Within a volatile world often verging on tragicomic apocalypse, Chester Himes's narrator in *Cast the First Stone* redeems himself from
the nameless chaos of prison life.

Chapter Four
Veil of Horror: *The Third Generation*

Chester Himes had traced his liberation from the cycles of prison absurdity in *Cast the First Stone*, a novel that had taken its regenerative title from John 8:7: "He that is without sin among you, let him cast the first stone at her." Similarly, Himes relied on biblical resonances as he wrote his next novel, *The Third Generation*: "I the Lord thy God am a jealous God, visiting the inequity of the fathers upon the children unto the third and fourth generation of them that hate me" (Exodus 20:5). A richly layered autobiographical novel, *The Third Generation* (1954) is the chronicle of an African-American family, the Taylors, from the nineteenth century through World War I. As autobiographical fiction, the novel is Himes's most poignant confrontation with his personal history and an incisive evaluation of the family as a center of cultural control.

Himes had started to write *The Third Generation* even as he revised the manuscript of his prison novel. Clearly *The Third Generation* emerged from the multiform complexities of Himes's own family history and the communal conflict between the Bomars and the Himeses. In June 1950, Himes and Jean had visited his brother Joseph, now a sociology professor at North Carolina College in Durham, and had taught a two-week course in creative writing. While staying with Joseph and his family in a pleasant house on Magnolia Street, Himes discovered "a number of pages of a manuscript that [his] mother had written about her family."[1] In *The Quality of Hurt*, he writes of his mother's manuscript: "Having nothing else to occupy her compulsive drive . . . Mother began tracing the history of her half-white family, the Bomars, out of slavery. It was from her notes that I got the idea for my semi-autobiographical novel, *The Third Generation*, but I didn't actually use any of her material—she was so closely related to the white planters, the Bomars and Clevelands, I didn't think the American public would accept it" (121). Himes's mother had died in Cleveland in 1945, before publication that year of *If He Hollers Let Him Go*. From the loving yet ultimately ambivalent memory of his mother and from his encounter with her newfound man·

script, Himes proceeded to fashion an authoritative work of autobiographical fiction.

That memory of his mother and her reincarnation in her family manuscript was the inspiration or the power engendering *The Third Generation* makes it tempting to ascribe Freudian redactions to Himes's novel.[2] Himes himself acknowledged this filial relationship: "The theme of the story concerns itself mostly with her abnormal love for her youngest and most handsome son and what it does to him by the time he reaches nineteen."[3] Even the novel's original title—*The Cord*—has Freudian resonances. The novel, however, takes its shape and power from the linear history of a black American family. It is prompted as much by historical necessity as personal experience. The evangelical citation that infuses the novel's title suggests that Himes, like his young avatar Charles in the novel, learns to see the world through a "veil of horror"[4] imposed by the cycles of family history.

The Taylor Family

The most immediate influence on the dialectics of African-American fiction is the family. Himes, seeking to appropriate and map his own family history in *The Third Generation*, evokes a definition of himself—a new name for himself—through an inquiry into domestic life. Ralph Ellison in "Hidden Name and Complex Fate" evaluates this unique naming ritual that is mediated by the black family: "We must learn to wear our names within all the noise and confusion in which we find ourselves. They must become our masks and our shields and the containers of all those values and traditions which we learn and/or imagine as being the meaning of our familial past."[5] In *The Third Generation*, the natural and unnatural laws of family life constitute a phenomenal universe, which the youthful protagonist must interpret before arriving at any moral truths about his identity in the world.

Charles Taylor is three and a half years old when *The Third Generation* opens and eighteen at its conclusion. The youngest of three sons and singled out as special by his mother because of his light skin, he apprehends at an early age that the family—his family—is the preserver and transmitter of culture. At the outset of the novel, he is in the background, a peripheral figure overshadowed by his mother, Lillian Taylor, yet molded by her. Mrs. Taylor provides the voice and narrative perspective in the opening chapters that condition the gradual emergence of Charles as a central figure in later sections of the novel. While his two brothers, William and Tom, who are five and eleven, respectively, at the start of the novel, work out their own separate peace with Mrs. Taylor, Charles must constantly discriminate among the conflicting elements in his mother's life, notably her twelve-year war with her husband, Professor William Taylor.

The struggle between Mrs. Taylor and Professor Taylor is for absolute authority over the destiny of the family. Husband and wife are perpetually at war with each other yet perpetually dependent on each other as well. They are constantly raging residents in Charles's consciousness, doing battle for the children's destiny. Even before the children understand the constituents of color, their parents embrace contrary notions about race that are at the heart of their conflict: "She wanted to rear them in the belief that they were, in large part white. . . . He wanted to prepare them for the reality of being black. Between them the battle of color raged continuously" (36). What constitutes the problem for this professional middle-class family at the turn of the century is the distaste Mrs. Taylor feels over her entrapment in a black world.

Race causes Mrs. Taylor to wander on the fringes of insanity throughout the novel. Yet it paradoxically turns her into a militant terrorist—to both her family and society. Mrs. Taylor, beautiful and light skinned, can journey on both sides of the color line. Obsessed with color, she asserts that she is "only one-thirty-second part Negro. And in her veins flowed some of the most aristocratic white blood in all the south" (11). Himes both mocks and laments Mrs. Taylor's dissatisfaction with two worlds: the black society that she views morbidly and attacks at every opportunity and a white world she persistently forces herself into but which will not acknowledge her. A demonic figure, she is so corrupted by racial contradictions that she views her husband's blackness from their first wedding night together, in a cheap, segregated hotel, as "the embodiment of evil" (25).

Professor Taylor, who is not the incarnation of evil but rather an increasingly harried and bewildered participant in marital discord, completes Himes's generic construction of the black family. He is a protean figure at the start of the novel, respected by students, liked by faculty colleagues, admired even by the governor of Mississippi. He has fine-tuned racial relations to a diplomatic edge, a man who, if left alone by his wife, would be content with his profession, his family, his soul, and his race. Yet persistently uprooted by family crises and driven irrevocably toward urban life, first in St. Louis and then in Cleveland (an odyssey paralleling the movement of Himes's own family), Professor Taylor gradually is alienated from his wife and from the environment his family finds itself in: "Professor Taylor had no ability at all for city life. At heart he was a missionary. He'd lived his life in southern negro colleges. There, a professor was somebody. He counted in the neighborhood. His family counted too" (159).

Charles, as participant-observer, presides over the constriction of family life and its convoluted decline. However, Himes embodies what could easily become representative narrative on the breakup of the black family with fresh expression. He insinuates into *The Third Generation* a vitality that springs from a sense of kinship. The family atmosphere often is "charged with strife and dissension" (42), yet Professor and Mrs. Taylor remain together almost until the end of the novel, when they finally divorce. Moreover, Charles maintains an ambivalent love-hate relationship with both his uncompromising mother and more easygoing father. Throughout the novel, the binding language of bloodlines is unquestionably central to the destinies of the parents and the children, as well as the shaping force of the narrative. Charles especially, that "third-generation" child out of slavery, fashions a self within the cultural archetype of family life. Even toward the end when his mother and father are divorced, diminished figures, the symbiotic family connection endures. Charles sleeps with his father in his father's bed in a one-room tenement; visiting his mother, he combs her hair. In the melodramatic denouement leading to his father's death, he makes a drunken attempt to protect his mother from a pimp, who in turn stabs his father.

The tableau in the hospital as Charles's father is dying is emblematic of the way all character and destiny in *The Third Generation* has been conditioned by family life:

At first he had eyes only for his mother. She stood beside the operating table with her back to the door, holding his father's hand. Her small, worn body was immobile, held in a posture of absolute faith. He knew that whatever the outcome, she had placed her trust in God. Somehow it was reassuring to see her thus.

Then he looked at his father. His nude black body lay passively on the white stretcher, almost as if resigned. His eyes were closed and the deep lines about his mouth and nose were relaxed. All of the signs of frustration had gone from his face and it was calm. There was a great dignity in his calm as if he had prepared himself to meet his Maker without excuses or deceit. (347)

That Charles's symbolic journey ends within this somewhat stiff and stilted family triptych suggests the paradigmatic power of kinship. The theological reverberations also remind readers of the curse hanging over this representative family whose members have come to see American realities through a veil of horror.

Myths of the Black Family

Although there is a dissolution of family life, notably toward the end of the novel, Himes does not subscribe to conventional notions of the matriarchal African-American family. Lillian Taylor might be the dominant partner, but Professor Taylor is the male head of the household, enjoying a middle- class occupation and often owning property. In fact, the children benefit from a double-headed household, whether living in rural or urban areas, and typically find ways to transcend the increasingly virulent domestic strife. Tom, the eldest son, is sent north to Cleveland to stay with Professor Taylor's kin and becomes a peripheral figure in the novel. William, following a school chemistry explosion that leaves him legally blind, enjoys special status as he moves up the academic ladder of respectability. Only Charles is a persistent witness to the interplay between the Taylor family and larger rural and urban realities.

To focus on the dysfunctional or disorganized aspects of family life in *The Third Generation* is to succumb to a pernicious set of assumptions, which can be traced from the pioneering work of E. Franklin Frazier to the Moynihan *Report* of 1965, on the instability of the African-American family.[6] The stability of the Taylor family is threatened as much by the pathology of Lillian Taylor as by the oppressive conditions of its environment. In this context, it is instructive to juxtapose the deathbed scene at the end of the novel with an early tableau as the Taylor family is on its way from Missouri to Mississippi, where Professor Taylor is to assume a new teaching post:

The hack contained three hard wooden seats, one behind the other, covered by a crude wooden top. Professor Taylor sat in the front seat, flanked by the two baby boys, while Mrs. Taylor and Tom sat behind. He picked up the reins and flipped them lightly across the gray backs of the mules. The team turned in the dirt square and headed away from town.

Beside the road were fields of corn already at full height, like rows of dark green sentinels in the soft dusk. No one spoke. They could hear the gentle rustle of the cornstalk in the faint breeze. Beyond a grove of white pines, a purple-orange cloud hung in the darkening sky . . . .

An atmosphere of serenity enveloped them. Mrs. Taylor dozed, too tired to take notice. Tom stared about him with bewilderment. He felt a vague sense of foreboding. William was soothed by the peaceful scene. But Charles was enthralled. The strange quiet beauty of the long green fields drew him into a state of enchantment. (44–45)

Here, in a superlative, sustained description of the rural South that continues for several pages, Himes creates a normative family model that is functional and culturally oriented. The Taylor family possesses strengths permitting it initially to combat the oppressive racial conditions of Mississippi during the World War I years.

The essential problem undercutting family life in *The Third Generation* is Lillian Taylor's refusal to see her family as a functional part of black society. Summarizing recent research on the African-American family, Jualynne Dodson emphasizes an emerging perception among social scientists that "black Americans' cultural orientation encourages family patterns that are instrumental in combatting the oppressive racial conditions of American society."[7] Mrs. Taylor does not fully apprehend this primal strength of the family, even as she is immersed in it, a raging, grotesque human force that constantly endangers her family's unity, stability, and security. For instance, early in the novel, Mrs. Taylor swears out an arrest warrant for her husband following an argument in which she had goaded Professor Taylor verbally in the most despicable manner and had been slapped in return. The scandal grows to such proportion that Professor Taylor has to resign his teaching post at a college in Missouri and seek another position. Earlier in their marriage, he also had been forced to resign as head of the mechanical department of the Georgia State College because of his wife's behavior: "She treated her husband with unwavering contempt and made enemies of all his associates. She whipped him with her color at every turn, and whipped all those about him. There came a time when she was not welcome in a single house. Yet her scorn and fury continued unabated. Eventually he was asked to leave the college" (28). Thus Mrs. Taylor unconsciously unleashes a violent assault on the very underpinnings of black family life—kinship with the community, education, and employment—that give it strength.

Despite Mrs. Taylor's disruptive and destructive behavior, the family remains tied to the black community. In Mississippi, where Professor Taylor teaches at yet another black college during World war I, there are even interludes of peace and pleasure, as when the family celebrates Christmas. Mr. Taylor's extended family system in Cleveland permits them to send their oldest son, Tom, north for a better education, while Mrs. Taylor supervises the education of Charles and William at home. In the college community Mr. Taylor feels himself an integral part of culture, teaching young people "to be proud of their racial heritage":

Professor Taylor liked it there. In spite of the indignities there was a certain inalienable dignity in the work itself, in bringing enlightenment to these eager young black people. . . . For what they learned, they and their mothers and fathers and sisters and brothers paid in privation, in Calico in January, cornpone diets and pellagra deaths. Professor Taylor was one of them, a little, short, black, pigeon-toed, bowlegged, nappy-headed man; he'd come from the same background with the same traditions; he was just more fortunate. He knew this, knew that he was more fortunate also in the selection of the mother of his sons. He wanted his wife to be happy, and his sons to grow up carrying the heritage of their race for better or worse. Only his wife was unhappy and hated it. And his sons hadn't yet learned that they were Negroes. (68–69)

Professor Taylor admires both the cultural values and the cultural distinctiveness of his environment, but Mrs. Taylor considers herself on a higher scale of class superiority. In short, they have competing perspectives on culture and on family life: one black and one disruptively nonblack.

Canonical Stories

As witness to the phenomena of family life, young Charles Taylor must contend with the emotional and ideological debates of his parents. He struggles to understand these phenomena, his own conflicting attitudes toward his mother and father, and the sociocultural context of his family life. Emerging slowly as the central consciousness in *The Third Generation*, Charles is the mask or veil for Chester Himes himself, who, on the eve of his departure for Europe, his exile from American soil, must wean himself from the family origins that had haunted him for so long.

The most impressive feature of Himes's first five novels is this conflation of autobiography and fiction—the recounting of parts of the author's life as structured stories. With *The Third Generation*, Himes reinvents the primal story of his own absolute origins within the interstices of family life. Characteristically he is both tantalized by a confessional impulse to trace his origins in a family descended from slavery and governed by the power of fiction to exorcise this impulse—to rise above the veil of horror. If, as Robert Stepto asserts, the "primary pregeneric myth for Afro-America is the quest for freedom and literacy,"[8] we can profitably view *The Third Generation* as Himes's most canonical text, a book in which he recasts the most personal genealogical materials in order to articulate or make literate both his bondage to and liberation from a racial past.

Through Charles, Himes manages to transmit intimate family details accumulated from the culture he was immersed in up to his nineteenth year: his mother's "light, lowly voice"; his father's anticipation of "summer's burning heat that charred him to a cinder"; his brother's blinding from the chemistry experiment explosion, leaving him "a stone of rigid tragedy in a field of barren loneliness." He seems intrigued by the notion that the life of a family is like a text giving rise to inspiration, to originality, to literacy. The Taylor family—the transubstantiated Himes family—is conveyed to us in images, episodes, and tropes that slowly and massively accumulate in power. Charles is the user of the language that constructs this family universe. As his own voice matures, he conveys the complexities his family faces as it contends with the dominant white social system.

When DuBois declared in *The Souls of Black Folk* (1905) that "the problem of the twentieth century is the problem of the color-line," he gave expression to a related canonical "story" or preexistent archetype that Himes, through his autobiographical character, Charles, must transcribe. Charles, who is bright, mercurial, secretive, stoical, and mystical, is a consciousness precluded by history. He is forced to confront the demonic contours of the color line—first by his mother's obsession with it, then by normal events of growing up in the South, and finally by his father's—indeed his family's—dispossession in the North because of it. Charles spends seven years coming to early consciousness in Mississippi. He is conditioned in part by the South's pastoral rhythms, depicted by Himes with superb attention to detail, as in the following passage on the advent of summer after the rainy spring: "In the rich steamy soil, seeds germinated like magic. Corn grew three inches high overnight. You could sit in the early sun and watch the grass come up" (74). This bucolic landscape, however, becomes demonic at its juncture with the color line. An irate white farmer in a mule-drawn wagon terrorizes members of the Taylor family, who are driving an automobile (a re-creation of an actual incident in the life of the Himes family). Another white man calls Professor Taylor a "nigger." Mrs. Taylor is arrested in Natchez for patronizing a white dentist. When she leaves briefly for Augusta with Charles and William, now nine and ten, respectively, to assume a teaching post, they are exposed to the indignities of traveling on a Jim Crow train. Each distressing racist incident undercuts the rhapsodic life of Charles, whose vital impulse to run wild through the southern landscape is distorted by the oppressive doom visited upon him by racist culture.

Charles, who prefers autonomy and reads for escape, an "Achilles in Mississippi" (129), nevertheless must create an identity for himself within a temporal succession of episodes embedded in the racist culture around him. In fact, much of *The Third Generation* is concerned with Charles's discovery that he is a historical being and his growing despair over this perception. When, after leaving Mississippi, for example, the family finds itself in Pine

Bluff, Arkansas, where Professor Taylor assumes yet another teaching post, the segregated world impinges on Charles's evolving life story: "The white world was sealed off. By comparison the colored world seemed shrunken and distorted, as if a specimen had been placed beneath an inverted microscope and had become strangely infinitesimal" (132–33). Gradually Charles discovers that he is not autonomous but rather that his identity and destiny are contingent upon a preexisting, closed system of racial relations.

Charles's dreams of childhood freedom are annihilated not only by a growing racial consciousness but more pointedly by the gunpowder explosion that ruins William's eyesight. Both brothers had been selected to perform this chemistry experiment at a school celebration, but Mrs. Taylor had punished Charles for his offensive language by not allowing him to participate. With her admonition, "God shall punish you," haunting him, Charles must watch from an auditorium seat as his brother loses control of the experiment and is engulfed by the explosion. This scene closely parallels the childhood disaster that befell Himes's brother Joseph in 1922 when the family was living in Pine Bluff. The episode leaves Charles—as it did Chester Himes—with a sense of shock that never wore off. Childhood illusions of freedom are literally and metaphorically blasted by a deeper and more startling recognition of the absurdity and complexity of the universe: "Before, life had held a reasoned pattern. There was good on the one side and bad on the other. And anyone could tell the difference. One knew what to expect. Good had its reward, and evil had its punishment. It had been that simple" (146). From adolescent autonomy, Charles—and indeed the family—falls into being a victim of capricious fate.

Thus the overarching canonical story in *The Third Generation* seems to involve God's will. What determines the structure and fate of the Taylor family is not exclusively the interplay of cultural forces or its situation in rural and urban areas but also a divine antecedent. God "visits ubiquity" into the generations that resist the religious ideals and ethos that should sustain families and communities. William's blinding is a prophetic forecast of the family's future. This is why Charles, at the end of the novel, sees how he was thrown out of the scheme of redemption by the capricious blinding of his brother: "He found himself thinking about Will's accident. That was the beginning, he thought, that was where it started. He thought about it for a long time, from the perspective of his horror; about his mother saying God was going to punish him for acting ugly, and how he'd thought about God afterwards when it had been Will who'd been blinded. Now he knew: *God didn't make a mistake, after all*" (349–50). This prophetic conflation of Charles's destiny and that of his family derives from the protagonist's haunting sense that their fate was ordered by God.

Street of Mirrors

The blinding of Will occurs at the exact midpoint of the novel and signals the final emergence of Charles as the central consciousness. In the first half of the novel, Charles felt himself autonomous. Now he—as did Himes himself—senses a reversal in power and fortune. Through semiautobiographical discourse and narrative, Himes explores and validates those self-determining episodes that destabilized his family and his childhood, first in St. Louis and then in Cleveland.

Despite family and cultural dissensions, Himes had described his childhood (through Charles) as paradisiacal and autonomous up to the blinding of Will. Following the accident, this paradisiacal sanctuary is replaced by a newer and stranger "contingent reality," as Frank Kermode puts it,[9] that is hard to articulate. In part, this semiautobiographical movement is from innocence to experience, from an Edenic paradigm to the modern paradigm of alienation. But it is also a movement from various familial and communal structures of security to the loss of identity in a strange, spiritless world. Charles's first winter in St. Louis is an emblem of his altered state:

A curious phenomenon took place within his mind that winter. Whole periods of his past became lost to recollection. There was no pattern, no continuity, no rational deletions, as the editing of a text. Fragments of days, whole months, a chain of afternoons were drawn at random, a word would be missing from a sentence he recalled with startling clarity, the intended meaning now gone. . . . It was as if a madman had snatched pages from a treasured book, the story stopping eerily in the middle of a sentence, a gaping hole left in the lives of all the characters, the senses groping futilely to fill the missing parts gone, now the meaning all distorted as if coming suddenly and unexpectedly into a street of funny mirrors. (162–63)

In this extraordinary passage, Himes reduces his adolescence to a disjointed text. Charles—the young Himes—is in a grotesque world of illusion, seeking some referent or linguistic structure by which he can make his identity intelligible.

As a mirror image of Himes, the protagonist, Charles, henceforth in the novel moves along a "street of funny mirrors" toward the shock of recognition that awaits him at the end. Charles's years in Cleveland—his family's diminished status and his parents' divorce, his difficulties in high school where he is only one of eight black students, his accident on the hotel elevator, his brief career at Ohio State, his lapse into crime and debauchery in Cleveland's ghetto—are now the nexus of Himes's own self-reflection. Formerly nurtured by a variety of interpersonal, familial, and social interactions, Charles now experiences a dissolution of the self, a growing nausea and revulsion. His all-consuming sexuality with the prostitute Veeny captures his primal motive: "He seemed floating in a nightmare of sensuality. Heat began growing in his brain in a thin steady flame. When he couldn't bear it he'd call her to bed. Each time he felt himself pairing out of himself into her as if giving her his life. He began to love the sensation of dying he derived from her" (332).

If *The Third Generation* is Himes's most confessional work, more so even than his autobiography, it is because we sense how closely he came to self-destruction. Through his persona of Charles, we see a youth struggling to piece together the dislocated fragments of his own life—the missing words and pages. "Finally he thought about himself" (350), declares Himes of his persona on the last page of *The Third Generation*. Charles plans to find out where an old girlfriend lives and to write to her, telling her everything. He also plans to say goodbye to his mother. Charles, as did Himes, will try provisionally to find a new language to structure his life. Chester Himes's vision narrowed in his fourth novel to the irreducible horror of a childhood and youth that almost consumed him. He creates a beautifully structured and controlled narrative of the eternal battle of the self caught between damnation and grace, and offers a tentative affirmation of his ability—if through no more than semiautobiographical art—to transcend cultural crisis and communal curse.

Chapter Five
Zoo Parade: *The Primitive, Pinktoes,* and *A Case of Rape*

One afternoon in 1956 Chester Himes was traveling on a Paris metro train. He had been in Europe since 1953 and had spent "forty-seven years on this earth" with little to show for it other than a suitcase and typewriter he was carrying with him. Suddenly Himes looked up from a picture of his German girlfriend Marlena to discover a middle-aged couple staring at him "with the lighthearted, wonderfully free interest of watching monkeys in the zoo, so common to the French" (*My Life of Absurdity,* 67). His life of absurdity had taken a new turn in exile, for now he had a heightened awareness of being perceived by French culture as an exotic, somewhat primitive African-American on parade.

As he describes it in *My Life of Absurdity,* Himes's encounter with the French couple is eerily reminiscent of a motif in the first book that he had completed while in exile. *The Primitive* had been released in paperback by New American Library in 1955 and published in French as *La Fin d'un primitif* by Gallimard in 1956 with a revealing preface by the author. In this novel, which traces the grotesque, Rabelaisian, ultimately macabre relationship between a black man and a white woman, the two lovers, Kriss Cummings and Jesse Robinson, sit placidly one morning after breakfast watching "Zoo Parade." Throughout the novel, they are also treated to the bizarre prophecies of another television personality, who happens to be a chimpanzee. *The Primitive,* still highly autobiographical, points in its surrealistic intensity to the absurd fictive universe that Himes would erect while in exile.

Himes's favorite novel, *The Primitive* aligns with two other novels he was working on in 1956 at the time he encountered the French couple. One, *Mamie Mason,* based on a minor character in *The Primitive,* is a robust satire on Harlem social life, which Himes depicts as a sexual jungle. Published in English as *Pinktoes,* the novel is Himes's only capricious treatment of interracial sex. With *Une Affair de viol* or *A Case of Rape,* which would not be published in France until 1963 and in the United States until 1984, four black men in Paris find themselves in another archetypal zoo, on trial for their lives, charged with the rape and murder of a white woman. With two novels set in New York and the other in Paris, *The Primitive, Pinktoes,* and *A Case of Rape* offer a profound, highly experimental assessment by Chester Himes of the combined, inherently grotesque forces of sexism and racism that he believed were governing the modern condition.

Serious Savage

In his interview with John Williams, Himes alluded to white readers' penchant both for exotic titillation and masochistic pleasure in their examination of literature by black writers. The dilemma for Himes as he began to write *The Primitive* was to avoid this facile emotional trap: "I want these people just to take me seriously. I don't care if they think I'm a barbarian, a savage, or what they think, just think I'm a serious savage."[1] Williams's shrewd insight later in the interview that *The Primitive* is a "brutal" book precisely because it assaults rather than titillates the emotions at all levels indicates the state of mind that produced this novel. The obsessive, almost hysterical sexuality that links Kriss and Jesse in a prolonged destructive embrace demands consideration of cultural symptoms and the racist pathologies that cause it.

Apparently Himes wrote *The Primitive* in an intense, unfettered state of mind. He described the process in a *New York Times Book Review* article:

The novel of mine which gives me particular pleasure is *The Primitive,* which I wrote in the summer of 1954, while living with an American white woman socialite, graduate of Smith College, descendant of the Pilgrims, in a state of near destitution in the House of the Bleeding Jesus on the hot, dirty square at the foot of the steps in Deya, Mallorca. . . . Believing that this cultured woman with whom I lived and the other white woman of whom I wrote were more primitive than I, it amused me to write this book, and it still amuses me to read it.[2]

The fragile Philadelphia socialite with whom he was living was Alva Trent. The woman about whom he wrote was Vandi Haygood, whom Himes had known at the Rosenwald Foundation during World War II and later at the Institute for International Education in New York. His "ardent affair steeped in sex and alcohol" (*The Quality of Hurt,* 136) lasted for eighteen months, from late 1951 to 1953. *The Primitive* was about this affair, and, prophetically, it foretells Vandi's untimely death. "In that book," Himes told Hoyt Fuller, "I was trying to show how ridiculous the whole case of racism was in America."[3] Using an interracial affair as a focus, Himes set out to demonstrate from a new perspective that remains largely autobiographical the absurdities inherent in the destructive confluence of sexism and racism in the American landscape.

The ironic presence of Alva reading his evolving manuscript and pulling him away from pornographic impulses apparently gave Himes an improvisational freedom. The book, Himes confesses, "acted as a catharsis," purging him of "all the mental and emotional inhibitions that had restricted [his] writing" ("Reading Your Own," 7). Clearly it would free him at last from the autobiographical impulse in fiction. At the same time, the metamorphosis of Himes into Jesse and Vandi into Kriss afforded the author the opportunity to transform potentially confessional titillation (Alva insisted that he tone down certain passages) into a coherent set of vital themes.

The psychological, political, and cultural contours of these themes were elucidated by Himes in his preface to *La Fin d'un primitif*. "In *The End of a Primitive*," he writes, "I have attempted to present an experience: to describe the idiocy of the twentieth century."[4] Himes posits that this idiocy of the age is provoked first by a dialectical clash between Christian ideals and capitalism and second by the irreconcilable opposition between our attempt to lead rational democratic lives and the presence of irrational political forces like McCarthyism in the contemporary political arena. From these inherent cultural contradictions there arises the schizophrenic mind, which manifests itself in a thousand ways.

Two manifestations of the schizophrenic mind are sexual and racial dissatisfaction. Himes describes a scenario much like the situation in Amiri Baraka's *Dutchman*: "In *The End of a Primitive*, I take a white American woman dissatisfied from the sexual point of view and a black American male dissatisfied from the racial point of view. These two types populate the United States like insects. I seal them hermetically in the apartment of the woman. I marinate them during a weekend in high-quality whiskey. This results in extravagance, buffoonery, idiocies and tragedy" (preface to *Fin d'un primitif*, 8). What else can be expected, Himes asks rhetorically, from a culture as chaotic as ours?

According to Himes, the modern white female and black male are new human species in the American environment. The black male derives his power from the way in which he serves as a catalyst for understanding moral, political, and historical contradictions. The white female is so powerful that she can save or destroy the world. She is the most privileged type in history, yet she is also the "most unhappy, the most incomplete, the least sure of herself and life, the most dissatisfied, above all from the sexual point of view, that has ever existed on earth." When such a type unites herself to the black American male, who is also a "bundle of psychoses," then fate reflects the "vulgarity and depravity" that our times seem destined to produce (9).

The key mistake that the white female makes in her approach to the black male is to view him as a primitive. In essence, Himes inverts conventional notions of primitivism and sophistication. In "Reading Your Own," he asserts that blacks are more sophisticated than whites: "We always know what white people are doing to us and what they are thinking while doing it. We are amused, in a masochistic sort of way, by their rationalizations and justifications. As my American negro protagonist in *The Primitive* consoles himself after killing his white paramour: 'Don't cry, son. It's funny, really. You just got to get the handle to the joke'" (8).

Himes enjoyed writing the extended joke—the catalog of absurdities—he was elaborating in *The Primitive*. At work with the rising sun, typing at the kitchen table with the "sweet, sensual, almost overwhelming scent of the lemon blossoms and the nearly unbearable beauty of the blossoming day" in the back of his mind (*The Quality of Hurt,* 302), Himes wrote slowly and steadily, savoring words and sentences, often sitting back to laugh hysterically at the evolving absurdities. Despite the idiocies he was exposing, the creation of *The Primitive* was "an exquisite act of love."

Race and Sex

In *The Quality of Hurt,* Himes observes that "the very essence of any relationship between a black man and a white woman in the United States is sex" (285). Himes's own life embodied this reality, and in his autobiography he confesses graphically to his sexual proclivities for white women: Vandi, Alva, Marlene, and Lesley, among others. As early as his first novel, *If He Hollers Let Him Go,* Himes was scrutinizing—specifically in the violent, almost libidinal conflict between the protagonist, Bob Jones, and the perverse racist coworker, Madge—this critical theme. In the words of one astute critic, Himes was inclined to view the underlying structure of American society "as an unresolved residue of erotic racial guilt."[5] This obsessive confluence of race and sex both engenders and reflects the absurdity of one's culture and one's time.

Himes in his fiction deliberately insists upon conflict and dualism in relationships between black males and white women rather than in racial and sexual regeneration. For example, although Lee Gordon, Himes's protagonist in *Lonely Crusade,* acknowledges that in Los Angeles "many interracial marriages had brought success and happiness," he is bereft of this possibility. Gordon's white mistress, Jackie, "made of him from the beginning just a beast to satisfy her sexual urges, or perhaps as therapy to ease her personal hurt." She reduces him to archetypal black potency, emasculating him, treating him as a fugitive primitive—herself the symbolic "female of the oppressors" (305).

By the time he began writing *The Primitive*, Himes was prepared to center an entire novel around this dialectic or counterpoint between race and sex and to utilize a range of grotesque techniques to expose the inane polarizations in American culture. He sets the action within a six-day framework, alternating the settings of the early chapters between Kriss Cummings's middle-class Gramercy Park apartment and Jesse Robinson's dingy tenement rooms in Harlem. They move separately and atomistically along two different cultural tracks—Kriss working and socializing, Jesse brooding over his failure as a novelist, contending with his fellow tenants, wandering the streets—until they meet, not having seen each other for several years, and stumble into a bacchanalian, increasingly nihilistic weekend at Kriss's apartment that ends with Jesse's murder of her. From the leisurely counterpointed early chapters, Himes moves cinematically to accelerated absurdist incidents within the closed, claustrophobic space of Kriss's apartment. His purpose is to reveal the contiguous psychic inanities of the two protagonists and the corresponding absurdities of a civilization they view through the television set. Himes's skill in juxtaposing grotesque tropes of inner domestic space and outer public space results in a narrative designed to express the ludicrous and lethal chaos provoked by discordant power relations in contemporary culture.

It can be inferred from the tight, almost classical structure of *The Primitive* that Himes wanted to employ form to circumscribe absurd events and exhaust existential relationships. Stephen Milliken observes that the novel's twelve chapters divide patently into three acts.[6] Act 1, comprising chapters 1–4, begins on a Tuesday early in April 1952, continues through the next day, and serves as expository background for two lives that are on the verge of psychic dissolution. These precarious lives converge when Jesse calls Kriss and they set up a Thursday evening date. Act 2, covering chapters 5–9, embraces the events of Thursday evening and Friday. During this period, Jesse and Kriss spend the night together but suffer larger defeats. Jesse learns that his third novel, *I Was Looking for a Street,* has been rejected. Kriss has a visit from Dave, who has rejected her for a woman of his own Jewish faith and is returning her keys. Act 3, constituting chapters 9–12 and running from Saturday to Monday morning, focuses on a saturnalian interlude at Kriss's apartment. There are random visits from decadent characters who carry their own hurts and who cannot interdict the tragic and concurrently absurd destinies of Himes's star-crossed lovers. Thus within the symmetrical structural units of *The Primitive*, Himes orchestrates a primitive asymmetry or unbalance in the tortured lives of two souls caught in a distinctly contemporary urban hell.

Himes is adept at structuring existential problems in *The Primitive* around juxtapositions and binary oppositions. The key elements in the existential predicament are expressed in sexual and racial terms that ultimately become embedded in the joined consciousness of Kriss and Jesse. The first nine chapters tend to oscillate between Kriss and Jesse, establishing a pathological parallelism in their lives that slowly overlaps and then inundates them. In the first chapter we see Kriss and sense the sexual disjunctions in her life. At thirty-seven, she is a superficially successful professional whose sexual life lacks a balance that typifies the other aspects of her existence. Divorced from a bisexual man, she has slept with at least eighty-seven men. Fair-skinned and beautiful, with blue eyes and blond hair, she is the paradigm of white woman—desired by men and women alike—for at work she is surrounded by female associates of ambiguous sexual proclivities.

Next, to establish the symmetrical pattern of Himes's novel, we see Jesse in chapter 2. Just as Kriss awakens on this bright April morning with a sense of panic, Jesse awakens—as had Bob Jones in *If He Hollers Let Him Go*—from a series of grotesque nightmares. In his last nightmare, his consciousness merges with that of a character in Gorki's "The Bystander" to reveal the extreme dissolution of this forty-one-year-old black writer's life: "Ah doan b'lieve dare evah wuz uh Jesse Robinson tah bagin wid!"[7] Jesse, like Kriss, is entombed in an apartment complex of grotesque and threatening contours. While Kriss must contend with the lesbian advances of Dot at work, Jesse has to deal with the homosexual Leroy, his lover, and even Leroy's ludicrously gay dog, Napoleon. Domicile and workplace are correlative cauldrons within which the two protagonists play out their absurd lives.

Himes has thrown a black man and white woman—two intelligent people—together on a grotesque modern stage, uniting them through alcohol and destructive sexuality in a macabre dance of death. There is both a pathetic and a ludicrous rhythm of emptiness to their marginal lives and relationship. Within the normally finite structures of classical tragedy and psychological realism, Himes locates those very irrational and absurdist phenomena—sexism and racism—that map so much of the "processed American idiocy" (22).

The "Teletonic" Age

Himes endows *The Primitive* with visionary humor by playing on the genre of futuristic fiction. The narrative action takes place in 1952, but it anticipates both Jesse's execution and the fate of the decade through the superimposition of media time for more mundane temporality. As Kriss bends over, naked, to flick on her television set, she encounters "the bright wide smile of a bleached skull and wreathed in that dreadful early morning cheerfulness of this teletonic age" (11). Wildly enchanted by television— this new electronic serpent in the garden—Kriss, and ultimately Jesse, discover that this new powerful medium transports them to the realm of grotesque revelation.

The skull that Kriss invokes on her twenty-one-inch screen is that of the moderator Glouchester who, with his sidekick, the Chimpanzee, is a parody of the celebrated 1950s talk show team of Dave Garroway and J. Fred Muggs. The chimpanzee is a grotesque shaman, possessing not only human voice but the power to divine the future. Within the absurd time warp that Himes deftly creates, the Chimpanzee, with its laughing face and bemused prophetic voice, offers a ludicrous gloss of the McCarthy era. The Chimpanzee looks into the very eye of cultural death, wryly establishing the political lineage of the era. Early in the novel, the Chimpanzee offers a typically ironic incantation:

Senator Richard M. Nixon of California will be nominated for Vice President, and on September 28, 1952, he will go on television—the same as you and I—to defend a political fund placed at his disposal by innocent and patriotic businessmen of California. . . . Mr. Nixon will also bare his financial status to the complete financial satisfaction of the Republicans and the complete dissatisfaction of the Democrats, after which he will hasten to the special campaign train of Republican nominee General of the Army, Eisenhower, to pose for a newsreel parody of the Jerry Lewis–Dean Martin comedy, "That's My Boy." (14)

Unencumbered by any anxieties (after all, he declares, he is only a monkey), the Chimpanzee offers with comic detachment a genealogy for the teletonic age: the election of Eisenhower, the ascendancy of McCarthy, the Civil Rights Act of 1954, the international intensification of racial conflict and colonial strife. The Chimpanzee is a bored primitive in the new media age; his "words" are ancestral warnings concerning the human condition that he defines and mocks.

Kriss, already addicted to television, initiates Jesse into this new age, dimly apprehending that the screen offers an act of self-definition. Future history that comes from the mouth of a Chimpanzee "with a condescending smile" (67)—that is, a record of calumnies and travesties in America, the Soviet Union, fascist Spain, South Africa, and elsewhere—flows from the television to the lives of Kriss and Jesse. The hypnotic prophecies of the Chimpanzee bring out in Jesse the heightened awareness of his absurd condition at a particular moment in history. To avoid being labeled a protest writer, he playfully suggests to Kriss that he will write a book about chimpanzees but upon mordant reflection concludes that there might be a "chimpanzee problem." In an obliquely comic way, Jesse discovers that the prophetic intelligence of the Chimpanzee is flowing through him, making of him a receptacle of history. During the weekend saturnalia, he tells a black editor who visits Kriss's apartment that he wants to write a new book, entitled *Gone with the Apes:* "I'm going to write the biography of a great white ape who rules all the black apes in the jungle. Mr. A as he is known to the black apes" (140). The inner screen of Jesse's own consciousness becomes illuminated by the wild visionary antics of the Chimpanzee—that transcultural "primitive" who obliterates conventional notions of time and place.

Primitivism and Decadence

Just as Himes comically undercuts conventional notions of the human and nonhuman with his talking, prophesying Chimpanzee, he also conflates stereotypical understandings of primitivism and civilization. Himes states in *The Quality of Hurt* that with *The Primitive* he was trying to say that "white people who still regarded the American black, burdened with all the vices, sophistries, and shams of their white enslavers, as primitives with greater morality than themselves, were themselves idiots" (285). Although the unrestrained alcoholism and distorted lusts of both Jesse and Kriss have a complementary character, the conclusion of *The Primitive* sustains Himes's satiric vision of the anarchic role that the black man must play when confronted with the almost mythic destructive force of white womanhood in Western civilization.

Jesse has unconscious knowledge of having killed Kriss with a knife; in fact, he fitfully naps beside her corpse in yet another macabre presentation of the dissolution in his protagonist's identity. Earlier that morning, Jesse had listened in a drunken stupor to the "prophetic chimpanzee" placidly describing the crime and his punishment—to be electrocuted in Sing Sing prison on 9 December 1952—but he had dismissed this knowledge with the sly allusion that this is what results from "reading too much Faulkner, son" (153). The "son" is Jesse's comic alter ego with whom he converses throughout the novel—the element that forces him to confront the absurdity of his "primitive" condition. At one point, making a haggard early morning return to his cluttered ever-threatening apartment, he talks with his comic counterpart about primitivism and civilization: "Can't eat bitter, son. No more than natural, anyway. Christian nation. Don't forget that. Pagans castrated all black slaves. Christians let them have families Christian way. Profit in it too. Don't forget the profit. More pops more pickaninnies sired. Just don't get bitter son. Remember it was business, strictly business. Funny, really. Funny as hell as you get the handle to the joke. Like the Englishman said to the cannibal, 'You eat me, you savage, but you'll pay hell digesting me'" (99). With the extraordinary juxtaposition of conflicting heritages and cultural elements in this passage, Himes comically indicts the West for its primitivism. At the same time, he undercuts any ability of the "savages" to digest the culture that has oppressed them.

Jesse's primitivism is not the romantic image conjured by white America but a dangerous, revolutionary nihilism that makes him a threat to oppressive and decadent Western civilization. Kriss, who stereotypes and sexually exploits black men, recognizes the threat that he poses: "If she could sleep with him and immediately afterward have him beheaded, she could enjoy his company" (57). Yet instead of being cannibalized sexually and killed by Kriss, Jesse inverts the archetypal conflict. He terminates all notions of a soft primitivism. He puts an end to the primitive through violence, and this revolutionary violence makes him paradoxically human (for now he must be taken seriously) and profoundly self-conscious of his absurdity.

Chester Himes in *The Primitive* expresses both cynical distrust of America and the comic, visionary thesis that black Americans can never genuinely transcend oppression except through suicidal rebellion. In a letter to John Williams from Yucatán, written probably in 1963, Himes expounds on the absurd, contradictory impulses governing the cultural landscape of the novel:

I wrote the PRIMITIVE sitting in the sun in the backyard in a house in Puerto de Pollensa and Deya, Mallorca, filled with tranquilizer pills, and everything was crystal clear and no more horrible than the life of Jesse from a distance of five thousand miles and five years (or in fact all life in America) and it amused me in the same grotesque morbid (if those are the right words) fashion which I would be amused seeing a white man who was chasing a Negro boy suddenly fall and break his neck. And it never occurred to me that Americans would find it objectionable—or any more objectionable than "normal" life in the U.S. taking place every day. In fact it always strikes me as funny (in a strange way) that white people can take the problems of race so seriously, guiltily, when they make these problems themselves and keep making them. It's like a man taking a rifle and shooting off his toes one by one and crying because it hurts.[8]

To an extent, Himes is Jesse (semiautobiographical passages in the novel would be recast in *The Quality of Hurt*), but he uses the grotesque to turn away from the confessional mode to underscore the cultural absurdities that prompt absurd private lives. Jesse and Kriss, in their extreme behavior, are not so much atypical as they are representative of cultural types unable to escape their sexual and racial pasts. Himes's talent in *The Primitive* was not to present these conventional themes with didactic seriousness but rather from the perspective—aided now by the author's expatriation—of a thinker bemused by his own prophecies of destruction.

Middle-Class Menagerie

With *Mamie Mason*, which he began to write in Paris early in 1956 while staying at the Hotel Royer-Collard, Himes suppressed temporarily the destructive impulse that had animated *The Primitive*. The converging themes of race and sex are still Himes's literary preoccupation, but *Mamie Mason* treats the subject from an almost whimsically improbable perspective. As Himes developed the manuscript, in rare good humor, *Mamie Mason* assumed the contours of a scatological romp. In February, he wrote to Carl Van Vechten that he had completed about sixty-eight pages of this novel but was satisfied with only a third of it (*My Life of Absurdity*, 23). Near the end of April he again wrote to Van Vechten: "I like the book, *Mamie Mason*, that I am trying to write. (I have written 120 pages and a separate 20 page introduction.) It is supposed to be humor, and I call it an experiment in good will. But I still don't know what I'm writing, although yesterday I could see the end" (*My Life of Absurdity*, 25).

Mamie Mason, which would not be published in English until 1961 by Olympia Press under the title *Pinktoes* and in French in 1962 by Plon, is a sexual romp in black and white through middle-class Harlem. Like all of his other novels to that point, it has autobiographical origins. Himes wrote to John Williams: "I wrote a satire on the Negro middle class in the frame of a story lampooning Mollie Moon. Mollie's husband, Henry Lee Moon, publicity director of the NAACP, is my cousin and I lived with them for a while in their Harlem apartment back in the 1940's."[9] The comically carnal heroine of Himes's novel, Mamie Mason, is patterned after this Mollie Moon, born

Mollie Lewis, whom the author had first visited in 1940—his first time in
New York—when he stayed at the Theresa Hotel.

In a second detailed autobiographical letter to Williams, Himes observed:

I suppose you know the story of how the 30-odd Negro writers and intellectuals
went to Russia in 1930 to make a film of the "Freeing of the Slaves." Henry and
Mollie were among the group, along with Langston, Loren Miller, Arabelle
Thompson, Ted Posten and others. Naturally these brothers could never do anything
together, so the Soveits [*sic*] got disgusted and sent them back home—or at least sent
them out of Russia. But instead of coming home, Mollie went to Berlin and stayed
four years and has always ever since been an authority on the rise to power of Hitler
and the Third Reich.

Anyway in 1940 Mollie and Henry lived in that fabulous apartment on West
66th Street (beside the stables) along with such characters as Ted Posten, Arabelle
Thompson, Katherine Dunbam, Eddie "Yale" Morrow, etc. Mollie tried to get
Richard Wright to come to a party she was giving for me, but Dick declined. . . .

I went to New York to live with Henry and Mollie Moon in their fabulous apartment at 940 St. Nicholas. It was during the time Roosevelt was running for his last
term. The Communists, the liberals, the Negroes, the negrophiles and friends were
getting together to elect Roosevelt. Henry Lee was working for the CIO Political
Action Committee—and Mollie was giving parties sponsored and paid for by various groups, including the Democratic National Committee. It was then and there
that I met everybody and came to know them well. There is hardly a prominent
middle class Negro of today I did not meet at that time—Walter White and co.,
Lester Granger, Ralph Bunche—oh hell, all of them. *It was from this time and from
these people I have taken scenes and characters for my book, MAMIE MASON
(Pinktoes in English).*[10]

Transformed into the ludicrous fleshpot of Harlem, Mollie's appearance as
Mamie Mason suggests just how savage Himes's personal invective could be,
even when cloaked in wild, fantastically absurd parody.

Caught up in a Parisian life-style that Himes himself found increasingly
absurd, the author transmuted much of this grotesquerie into his evolving
manuscript of *Pinktoes.* His "exercise in goodwill" is a buoyant and ribald satire on the celebrities, movers, and bluebloods (the "Talented Tenth") of the
Harlem social register and the white potentates and luminaries who visit
them—ostensibly to promote civil rights but in reality to avail themselves of
the primitive orgies sponsored by Mamie Mason. The novel's comic heroine,
Mamie, is a sensual and voluptuous thirty-nine-year-old society matron—
Harlem's foremost hostess. With her husband, Joe Mason, a philandering
civil rights director, she lives at 409 Edgecombe Avenue, an address that

Himes chose deliberately to heighten the social satire. Since the 1930s this Sugar Hill apartment complex had been the most prestigious address in Harlem. One social historian notes:

During the thirties and forties, the tenants of 409 Edgecombe Avenue included W.E.B. DuBois, William Stanley Braithwaite (poet and critic), William T. Andrews (State Assemblyman), Roy Wilkins and Walter White (officials of the N.A.A.C.P.), Charles Taney; Aaron Douglas (painter), Pearl Fisher and Ivy Fisher (sister and widow, respectively of novelist Rudolph Fisher), Josh White (folk singer); Thurgood Marshall, William Melvin Kelly, Sr. (a former editor of the *Amsterdam News*), Mercer Ellington (musician), and Elmer Carter and Ellen Tarry (journalists). At fourteen stories high, 409 was also the tallest building on the Hill, and Walter White's apartment, on the thirteenth floor, was known as the White House of Harlem, because of the many notables from the worlds of politics, literature, and theatre who were entertained there.[11]

Himes's vision of Harlem would darken, but his first Harlem domestic novel captures with parodic intent the vivacity and excitement of an older Harlem that was rapidly fading even as Himes set his novel there in the mid-1950s.

Pinktoes, which Olympia Press published in 1961 apparently in order to capitalize on the earlier success of *Lolita,* is a jumble of comic episodes and vignettes on Harlem. Rarely in complete control of his comic materials, an admission the author makes in his autobiography, Himes nevertheless creates a memorable portrait of Mamie Mason as Harlem society's heroine. An apostle of interracial loving as the solution to the "Negro Problem," Mamie's celebrated "race relations" parties and balls devolve typically into interracial sex circuses. Before Mamie, white and black dignitaries find themselves literally or symbolically stripped naked and offered as votaries to be consumed by her injunction, "More interracial intercourse." Harlemites and their distinguished white visitors from America's centers of power—politics, publishing, education, the arts—engage in a prolonged carnival or bacchanalia that Himes treats typically as a joke. The lesson that history teaches is that Harlem is "an excursion in paradox" and that the only "solution" to the paradox of race relations there or anywhere else is not so much sex as laughter. The people of Harlem are "laughing at the white people and laughing at themselves, laughing at the strange forms injustice takes and at the ofttimes ridiculousness of righteousness."[12]

Through satire and broad slapstick, Himes persistently deflates any prospect of Harlem or its celebrated Mamie serving as a laboratory where racial problems can be solved. Attentive as she is to the small black notebook in which she keeps the names of visiting celebrities, Mamie is far too buffeted by gargantuan passions to serve as a proper ambassador of race relations. Mamie's dieting, her key stratagem of social, sexual and racial advancement, is undercut by her eating binges. Himes's hyperbolic descriptions of Mamie's culinary passions constitute some of the finest passages in *Pinktoes*:

At two-thirty that afternoon, hunger awakened Mamie Mason. She rushed to the kitchen, gulped a half bottle of skimmed milk, ate six raw eggs, a half pound of raw, partly frozen ground steak, two all beef frankfurters, and six slices of boiled ham after peeling off the fat. Suddenly she was sick. She drank a stiff bourbon straight to keep it down, but it kept coming up and she just made it to the bathroom to let it go. After it had all gone she took a tablespoon of mineral oil, returned to the kitchen, ate three hard-boiled eggs, two slices of dry toast, a can of tunafish, and a head of iceberg lettuce sans dressing. Everything stayed down. She mixed a Scotch highball and took it to her bedroom. Then she went to the bathroom and swallowed two tablespoons of milk-of-magnesia laxative. (75)

Mamie is so obsessed with visceral needs that she contemplates changing her annual masked ball, the high point of Harlem social life, to a ham bake: "Everyone was running about talking about interracial relations and desegregation and the like when the fact of the matter, when you came right down to it, the only real solution to the Negro problem was ham" (209).

In his evocation of Harlem U.S.A. in *Pinktoes,* Himes reduces the culture of this city within a city to a satiric sexcapade. His interracial gallery of sexual grotesques does not constitute any positive social force, nor is interracial sex ever presented as a serious stratagem for racial advancement. Himes obviously had fun depicting the buffoons populating Mamie Mason's universe. In face the Harlem of *Pinktoes* has an almost disembodied innocence to it, as though Edgecombe Avenue and its denizens constitute another world. Yet even as he was completing the manuscript of *Pinktoes* in 1956, Himes was working at the theme of interracial sex from a grimmer international perspective.

Caged Victims

With *A Case of Rape,* Himes continues to be preoccupied with the destructive elements of sexism and racism in contemporary culture but now on an international scale. As an expatriate writer, Himes thought that he had to write about France's place in the history of racial exploitation. Moreover, from the center of civilization itself, Paris, Himes wanted to confirm the pre-

Socratic notion that *ethos* is *daimon*—that character is fate. The Paris court-room drama framing *A Case of Rape* illuminates the absurd, inevitable fates of four black Americans and a white woman whom they are accused of having raped and murdered.

Himes's strong insistence on treating the contemporary situation from an absurdist perspective dominated his conception of *A Case of Rape*, as well as the farcical novel he was writing at the same time, *Mamie Mason*. As Himes describes the situation in *My Life of Absurdity:*

I was finding it so difficult to keep *Mamie Mason* funny that I began writing the syn-opsis for an epic novel about the American blacks in the Latin Quarter which was eventually published as a novel, *Une Affair de Viol*. Everyone except me realized the writer in the story, who set out to prove that four blacks charged with rape were as unlikely to commit rape as the prime minister of England, was absurd. All blacks are likely to rape a white woman. They are just as unlikely to be accused of it. Because of this, French police are less likely to accuse a black of raping a white woman than American police are. By this reasoning French police have carved the reputation of being liberal. All the life around me was interracial, bizarre and absurd. (38)

In quarrying material for this new novel, Himes was once again subjecting his characters to primal racial and sexual impulses that render their lives absurd. The austere economy of each of the fifteen chapters in *A Case of Rape* permits Himes not only to expand his grotesque universe beyond the American envi-ronment but also to render with astonishing mythological power some un-happy truths about the volatile clash between primitivism and civilization.

A Case of Rape is an experimental type of moralized fable of the absurd that delineates the limits of knowledge governing a community. It is a thriller not so much in the mode of the Harlem detective fiction that Himes would soon begin to write but in the sense that it explores the opaque ways in which we force sexuality and race to consciousness. Thus *A Case of Rape* is, for both readers and the "investigator," an American black writer named Roger Garrison who wants to prove an "international conspiracy of racism," a problem in perception.[13]

The case opens in Paris, a symbolic Western community beset by critical relations between social classes and by the unnerving impact of the Algerian War. It is a marginally coherent community—one still ordered and ruled provisionally by law. Each brief chapter bears a title ("The Change," "The Defense," "The Summations," "The Verdict," "The Sentence," "The Fourth Estate," to cite the first six) that confirms the uncertainty of crude judicial power and process as the determinant of particular social relationships, with a sort of documentary irony that has no antecedent in Himes's fiction. Himes establishes the judicial "facts" in the initial chapter: "Testimony was presented by the instruction judge to the effect that Mrs. Elizabeth Hancock Brissard accompanied Scott Hamilton to his hotel room at three o'clock of the afternoon of Sunday, September 8th" (3). Hamilton had had an affair with Hancock that had ended amicably, and now they were together to work out an arrangement on a novel that they had collaborated on. (Himes and Alva had written a novel together, *The Golden Chalice,* which was never published.) At Hamilton's apartment, they were joined by three other "American Negroes": Caesar Gee, Theodore Elkins, and Sheldon Edward Russell.

Some three hours later, a French couple across the courtyard witnessed a struggle. "It appeared to them as though Mrs. Hancock was trying to prevent the four Negro men from pushing her from the open window" (6). Later her bruised body is found dead. The faces of Russell and Hamilton are scratched and bloody. An autopsy reveals that Mrs. Hamilton had had sex at least four times within twelve hours preceding her death. Traces of cantharides were in her blood. After a summary trial, the four defendants are convicted of rape and murder and are sentenced by the French court to life imprisonment. Himes narrates the powerful, chaotic forces underlying this episode within the framework of a detached, almost clinical deposition. Ironically the legal system becomes the last bastion against "that uncharted wilderness—that dark pathology of lust and hate—of interracial motivation" (23).

Uncharted Wilderness

The African critic Ambroise Kom is fundamentally correct in asserting in his study *Le Harlem de Chester Himes* that *A Case of Rape* "confirms in another manner the primitivism of the Negro."[14] However, it is the faulty white and black perceptions of this primitivism that preoccupy Himes in his novel. What he finds abhorrent—and treats satirically—is a collective racist cult of primitivism that both obscures the authentic existence of black people and thwarts interracial love.

Unlike other expatriates, Himes was under no delusions that the French were less racist than Americans. In a 1962 letter to John Williams from Paris, he refers to a piece that he wrote for *Candide* "in which I compared the U.S. racists to the French OAS; I said basically the only difference was that the U.S. racists were going to win and the French racists [*sic*] OAS lose."[15] More pointedly in an April 1960 letter to Margrit de Sablomere, the author declares that *A Case of Rape* was written "in order to emphasize the preconceptions and humiliations that Black Americans were subjected to in Paris during the Algerian war."[16] Western racism invalidates justice, humanity, and the possibility of love between men and women. It provokes absurd strategies for rationalizing racial and sexual cruelty.

Because of the fundamentally racist and sexist environment depicted in *A Case of Rape*, its characters are fated to have flimsy, self-conscious egos. They are exiles and aliens—strangers in a strange land—and are mordantly self-conscious about race and sex. As Calvin Hernton observes in his postscript to the American edition of *A Case of Rape,* "Collectively, the four defendants, as well as Roger Garrison, show that they are held hostage by the interplay of the racist and sexist elements within themselves" (126–27). Race and sex—the twin loci of the uncharted modern wilderness—are the constituents not only of identity but of power.

Himes uses his characters allegorically to discourse on these twin constituents of race and sex. Caesar Gee, twenty-nine years old and in Paris for four years, the son of a father made rich by the numbers racket, is "small, dapper and black" (35). With his black face, mustache, and goatee, he is a radical exhibitionist—Rabelaisian, self-indulgent, provocative. He resides at the Hotel George V, parades in a yellow Cadillac, and promenades with a white borzoi. Sheldon Russell, thirty-five, who holds forth at Café Tournon (as did Himes's friend Ollie Harrington) has "tremendous pride in his own heritage" (42). Harvard educated, married twice and divorced from white wives, he is now a slave to upper-class white women—a "dilettante Uncle Tom" (47). Theodore Elkins, the youngest of the defendants at twenty-four, also possesses "race-conscious dignity" (48) and is quick to anger. A student at the Sorbonne "studying political science in view of seeking his career among the newly emerging African states" (52), he is engaged to a white American professor six years his senior. Scott Hamilton, the oldest defendant at forty-six, "is the only one who did not like Paris. He had never found anywhere that he liked, and now he never would" (54). He is, although skillfully camouflaged with fictive biographical elements, a mask for Himes himself. All "revere" white women.

Scott's affair with Elizabeth Hancock, which begins in 1953 aboard a ship bound for Europe, is a thinly veiled treatment of Himes's affair with the "Alva" of his autobiography. They are matched allegorically, with Scott descended from the Hamiltons and Fairfaxes and Elizabeth from John Hancock and the Pilgrims—a mythological conflation of the American ethos. Juxtaposed against this New World amalgam is the Old World husband she tries to escape, André Brissaud, who is "embued with an ingrown refined evil of generations of decadence" (76). Scott and Elizabeth (they serve as the title for chapter 12) are the new American Adam and Eve. They try to enact a pastoral dream together. They need to save and rehabilitate each other. Scott sees in Elizabeth a "casualty of racism—an inverted sort of racism that perpetuates the dominance of the male" (83). Inevitably the dream fades as they rediscover that they are caught in a maze of sexual and racial barriers.

Clearly Himes, in this brilliant, experimental novel, wants to distill the history of civilization into a struggle between sexual drives and the social controls and taboos designed to control them. The sexual liberation of the principals in this allegorical drama is fated to collide not only with their own limitations but with social repressions and inhibitions. Roger Garrison, whose name suggests the abolitionist crusader, who would "liberate" sexuality and race from an international capitalist conspiracy, is limited by facts— which only Himes provides editorially in the thirteenth chapter, "The Missing Evidence."

Missing Evidence

Roger Garrison is the "investigator" of the sexual and racial jungle Himes outlined. Given his preconceptions and foibles, he is a blind man in a cage, another specimen in Himes's zoo parade. As an "American Negro writer" with a white wife and two children, he is obviously a parody of Richard Wright. (The tenuous friendship between Wright and Himes was shattered by this parody.) Intent on uncovering an international conspiracy designed to prove that blacks are inferior, Garrison is not interested in the guilt or innocence of the defendants or the authentic relationship to Mrs. Hancock.

The withheld evidence that Himes insinuates into his narrative suggests that we all assume complicity in the distortion of race, gender, and sexuality in the modern world. It is only partially correct to indict culture for promulgating repressive differentiations. Equally evident is our own power to incite and sustain these oppressive categories. Elizabeth went to Hamilton's apartment in a state of physical and emotional exhaustion and mental imbalance. Previous to her meeting with Scott, she had been with her husband who, surreptitiously inciting her with Spanish fly, had engaged her in a sexual orgy. Then while meeting with Scott to reconcile publishing problems with their novel (problems, Himes infers, that were precipitated by Roger Garrison), she again is secretly administered cantharides in wine—this time by the "racially-inspired *spite*" (98) of Ted, who is also observed by a conspiratorially quiet Shelly Russell. Such incitement, both self-induced and administered malignantly, suggests that the mechanisms of power and control reside darkly in all beings. As Himes asserts cynically at the end of *A Case of Rape*, "We are all guilty" (105).

The French critic Michel Fabre cogently states that "*A Case of Rape* is the chronicle of a love destroyed, absurdly made impossible by the cultural odds against it."[17] The tender love that had existed between Scott and Elizabeth was amazing to Himes by virtue of the very fact that it did exist within a culture governed by intense biases. Together Scott and Elizabeth could provisionally inhabit "a dark void of peace beyond escape, free from all the anxieties and hurts and demands of her race and culture" (85). In this timeless void, they constitute their own unitary power, a forceful procreative reality. Yet they can never transcend social controls. They too ultimately are swallowed in the racial and sexual labyrinth of society. Ironically Roger Garrison was correct: the thrust of civilization is toward control of our sexual and racial destinies. These are the constituents of our fate, the genealogy governing our lives in an absurdly disciplinary, legalistic world.

Chapter Six

The Greatest Show on Earth: The Detective Fiction

Following his three novels tracing the vagaries of interracial sex—*The Primitive, Pinktoes,* and *A Case of Rape*—Himes abandoned both the confessional mode and conventional novelistic genres to erect a radically new fictive universe. Refining the absurd elements inherent in his confessional fiction, Himes created a series of novels centered almost exclusively in Harlem and dealing with the criminal world. With the gradual development of his archetypal black detectives, Coffin Ed Johnson and Grave Digger Jones, he would devise an entirely new crime fiction genre—or antigenre—that places the black experience in America in a new ideological context.

When Jesse in *The Primitive* observes, "Good thing I read detective stories; wouldn't know what to do otherwise" (160), he offers an uncanny prophecy of the fictive mode that Himes would embark upon for Marcel Duhamel's famous "La Série noire." Himes himself had read crime and detective fiction since his days as a young convict. In the early 1930s he had published his crime stories in *Esquire* and *Abbott's Monthly.* And he had subscribed to *Black Mask,* the foremost detective pulp of the era.[1] Thus when Duhamel suggested to Himes that he read Dashiell Hammett and Raymond Chandler, whose early work had appeared in *Black Mask,* Himes knew what the editor meant. By 18 January 1957, Himes had completed his first novel in a new genre, titled initially *The Five Cornered Square,* in French *La Reine des pommes* (Gallimard, 1958), and finally in English, *For Love of Imabelle* (Fawcett, 1957). For more than ten years, the expatriate author would have Harlem on his mind, creating a unique cycle around what he laconically termed on the dust jacket of the best-known novel in the series, *Cotton Comes to Harlem,* his "Harlem domestic stories."

Starting from Harlem

Harlem begins where Central Park West becomes Eighth Avenue at 110th Street, the junction known as Frederick Douglass Circle. For years a signpost at this junction was misspelled Frederick Douglas Circle—the dropped second *s* providing an ironic twist to a visitor's entrance into the "black capital of the world." Central Harlem, bounded by 110th Street on the south, Third Avenue on the east, the parks along St. Nicholas, Morningside, and Manhattan avenues on the west, and the Harlem River on the north, was a world that Chester Himes would re-create from memory. Out of the "pure homesickness" of the exile, Himes went back to both a real and an archetypal realm of America, happily creating "all the black scenes of my memory and my actual knowledge."[2]

How did the real and mythopoetic landscape of Harlem come to dominate the literary imagination of Chester Himes? Returning to New York in 1955 at the age of forty-six to reedit *The Primitive* for New American Library, Himes had resided at the Hotel Albert in Greenwich Village. He visited often with Van Vechten at his apartment on Central Park West. One night at Van Vechten's, he met the Jamaican writer George Lamming, author of the contemporary classic *The Castle of My Skin,* and from there they went to the Red Rooster restaurant on Seventh Avenue in Harlem. He reports: "I discovered that I still liked black people and felt exceptionally good among them, warm and happy. I dug the brothers' gallows humor and was turned on by the black chicks. I felt at home and could have stayed there forever, if I didn't have to go out into the white world to earn my living" (*My Life of Absurdity,* 23). Randomly Himes absorbed the typography of Harlem—its streets and sections, from the bleakest ghetto in the "Valley" to elegant Edgecomb Avenue in Sugar Hill and Strivers Row on 138th and 139th streets, its cultural landmarks like the Hotel Theresa (Harlem's Waldorf Astoria), Blumstein's Department Store, and Small's Paradise; the haunts of its legendary figures like Father Divine and Marcus Garvey. Even the mundane bars, beauty parlors, tenements, police precinct houses, nightclubs, theaters, churches, funeral parlors, offices, and stores seemed to raise a question of identity for Himes. "Inadvertently, it was then I learned so much about the geography of Harlem, the superficiality, the way of life of the sporting classes, its underworld and vice and spoken language, its absurdities, which I was to use later in my series of Harlem domestic stories" (*My Life of Absurdity,* 25).

In *My Life of Absurdity,* Himes confessed that he "really didn't know what it was like to be a citizen of Harlem." He had "never worked there, raised children there, been hungry, sick or poor there." He then underscores a crucial point: *"The Harlem of my books was never meant to be real; I just wanted to take it away from the white man if only in my books"* (126). Focusing on Harlem, Himes sensed an ideological shift as he explored a largely black universe, not with any intention of offering a slice of life or conventional artistic verisimilitude but rather with the goal of uncovering the absurdity that he had come to believe was the essence of the black condition. "Realism and absurdity are so similar in the lives of American blacks," asserts Himes, "one cannot tell the difference" (109).

The Harlem that Himes began to explore in *The Five Cornered Square* (subsequently *For Love of Imabelle*), the first of the crime novels that he wrote concurrently with *Mamie Mason (Pinktoes),* has its recognizable geography, but the author is far more interested in the metaphysical dimensions of his grotesque landscape. Himes declares in *My Life of Absurdity,* "It was not *Mamie Mason* but *The Five Cornered Square* that was the logical follow-up to *The End of The Primitive*" (111). The strange, violent, unreal world of *For Love of Imabelle* is the arena or perhaps corollary for equally grotesque inhabitants of this locale. From the onset of his crime fiction, Harlem is a world where pandemonium reigns, whether at the Savoy Ballroom (which would be closed in 1958 and subsequently torn down to accommodate an urban renewal project), inside a precinct house, on the street, or in a sleazy bar. It is a world of distortions, dissolution, and chaos: "Looking eastward from the towers of Riverside Church, perched among the university buildings on the high banks of the Hudson River, in a valley far below, waves of gray rooftops distort the perspective like the surface of the sea. Below the surface, in the murky waters of fetid tenements, a city of black people who are convulsed in desperate living, like the voracious churning of millions of hungry cannibal fish. Blind mouths eating their own guts, stick in a hand and draw back a nub."[3] This is not so much a faithful rendering of scene as an expressionistic reconstruction of reality designed to uncover the bizarre and macabre mechanism of an inner city.

A similar cannibalism pervades the settings of *Baby Sister*, a film scenario that Himes wrote in 1961 "while living in a one-room penthouse atop a five-floor walk up overlooking the *Ramparts* in the 'old town' of Antibes."[4] Termed by Himes a "black Greek tragedy" but in actuality a contrived, maudlin, and melodramatic tale of an archetypal teenager, Baby Sister, the stereotypical symbol of black female sexuality, and her ability to create sexual chaos among her black and white suitors, the scenario is set in a primordial urban jungle: "This is Harlem, U.S.A., a city of contradictions. A city of Negroes isolated in the center of New York City. A city of incredible poverty and huge sums of cash. A city of the meek and the violent. A city of brothels, bars, and churches. Here is the part called Sugar Hill, where the prosperous live—the leaders, the professionals, the numbers barons. Here is the part called the Valley, where the hungry eke out an existence and prey upon one another. The Valley is like a sea filled with cannibal fish" (*Black on Black*, 7). Baby Sister is a "juicy, tasty lamb in a jungle of hungry wolves," fit prey to be devoured.

The strict demarcations of this infernal Harlem landscape are apprehended by the white detective Brock in *Run Man Run* (1966), originally published as *Dare-Dare* by Gallimard in 1959, and a grim, superlatively conceived crime novel that is unique in that it does not feature Coffin Ed Johnson and Grave Digger Jones:

> As Brock drove slowly in the stream of northbound traffic he had a fleeting image of the city in the stomach of a cloud. It was a clean and peaceful and orderly city being slowly consumed.
>
> But when he came into Harlem at 110th Street and turned west on 113th Street the image suddenly changed, and now it was the image of a city already consumed with only bits of brick and mortar left to remind one that there ever had been a city. (*Black on Black*, 11)

Here the cannibalism inherent in the earlier description from *For Love of Imabelle* is replicated with the pictorial playfulness of a Chagall canvas, the apocalyptic emptiness of Ensor.

In fact, the sense of apocalypse—whether in fire or ice—is the most dominant impression generated by Himes's Harlem universe. The climate of his nine Harlem crime novels does not admit any relief or moderation in violent extremes of weather. Four novels in the cycle—*For Love of Imabelle* (1957), *The Real Cool Killers* (1959), *All Shot Up* (1960), and *Run Man Run* (1966) —transpire in frozen urban terrain. In counterpoint, five of the "domestic" novels—*The Crazy Kill* (1959), *The Big Gold Dream* (1960), *Cotton Comes to Harlem* (1965), *The Heat's On* (1966), and *Blind Man with a Pistol* (1969)—are set in the sweltering, claustrophobic months of summer, typically July. The physical landscape of Harlem seems infernal. For example, in *The Heat's On,* one of the most outrageously grotesque novels in the series in which Coffin Ed and Grave Digger search for $3 million worth of heroin, there is no escape from the demonic heat: "Even at past two in the morning, The Valley, that flat lowland of Harlem east of Seventh Avenue, was like the frying pan of hell. Heat was coming out of the pavement, bubbling from the asphalt, and the atmospheric pressure was pushing it back to earth like the lid on a pan."[5] In Himes's Harlem, the weather is an expressive vehicle that heightens the hellish pandemonium typifying a nihilistic world.

Climate in Himes's Harlem novels merely confirms the chaotic disruptions in the inhabitants' lives. Landscape and climate mirror and flatten an alienating culture. Describing in *Cotton Comes to Harlem* a grim area on Eighth Avenue near 112th Street, Himes writes:

This was the neighborhood of the cheap addicts, whiskey heads, stumblebums, the flotsam of Harlem, the end of the line for the whores, the hard squeeze for the poor honest laborers and a breeding ground for crime. Bland-eyed whores stood on the street corners swapping obscenities with twitching junkies. Muggers and thieves slouched in dark doorways waiting for someone to rob; but there wasn't anyone but each other. Children ran down the street, the dirty street littered with rotting vegetables, uncollected garbage, battered garbage cans, broken glass, dog offal—always running, ducking and dodging. God help them if they got caught. Listless mothers stood in dark entrances of tenements and swapped talk about their men, their jobs, their poverty, their hunger, their debts, their Gods, their religions, their preachers, their children, their aches and pains, their bad luck with the numbers and the evilness of white people. Workingmen staggered down the sidewalks filled with aimless resentment, muttering curses, hating to go to their hotbox hovels but having nowhere else to go.[6]

Himes's two detectives would pave over this Hogarthian scene and turn white people—the perpetuators of a repressive bourgeois culture—to hogs for having produced it. This is the landscape of nightmare, of hell, far removed from Edgecombe Avenue, not to mention white Manhattan, that Coffin Ed and Grave Digger must mediate their way through and attempt to subdue. It is a demonic world, a dark ghetto confirming Kenneth Clark's astute observation: "the ghetto is ferment, paradox, conflict, and dilemma."[7] More like bedraggled wild men than rational detectives, enraged exiles within their own community, Grave Digger Jones and Coffin Ed Johnson seek meaning in a strictly absurd and ludicrously disruptive community.

Genre and Antigenre

That Himes breaks new ground by setting his detective fiction in Harlem makes it impossible to read his work in this genre without apprehending that he transforms conventional reader expectations. He asserts in *My Life of Absurdity* that when he began writing the first of his crime novels, *For Love of Imabelle*, he felt "that this wasn't a detective story," that he "didn't know how to write a detective story" (111). Indeed the famous Harlem detective team of Coffin Ed Johnson and Grave Digger Jones does not appear until the eighth chapter of the novel, and then only after Himes's editor, Marcel Duhamel, had told him, after perusing the first eighty pages of the manuscript, that Himes could not write a *policier* novel without police. Nevertheless, Himes realized that he was breaking new ground in a world of crime fiction that previously "had been the strict domain of whitey" (120). Himes was thus somewhat disingenuous when he told John Williams that with his crime fiction he was "just imitating all the other American detective story writers," that he simply took the "straightforward violence" of the genre and its plain narrative form and "made the faces black."[8] In essence, Himes took the critique of culture inherent in the tough-guy or hard-boiled detective fiction of Chandler, Hammett, and other writers of the 1930s and 1940s and transformed the genre into an absurdist parody of the search for order and values in a capitalist and racist world.

In this connection, we must acknowledge that classic hard-boiled American detective fiction emerged from the turbulence of the Great Depression. Similarly Himes began his detective series at a point in American history when the absurdities of racism and oppression would give rise to the civil rights movement, black nationalism, and the urban riots of the 1960s. Himes's two detectives descend from the hard-boiled tradition of the 1930s popularized first by Hammett's Sam Spade, a cynical, unsentimental detective swimming in a sea of urban crime. In *The Maltese Falcon,* Spade becomes a prototype for many later outsiders who attempt to reestablish justice in a chaotic cultural period, notably Chandler's Philip Marlowe, Mickey Spillane's Mike Hammer, and Ross Macdonald's Lew Archer. Himes, however, refined and heightened certain contradictions inherent in the genre. As Edward Margolies asserts, "The hardboiled genre is a peculiar mix, celebrating American individualism while at the same time denigrating the corruption of American society."[9] More than his predecessors, Himes uses his two detectives not so much to solve crimes and preserve order as to test the impossibility of sustaining meaning in a sociocultural world that is inherently irrational and absurd. Thus Himes's detective fiction appears in a new critical light as a comic antigenre in which the "crime" derives from a capitalist world fragmented by racism and economic exploitation. In the end, Grave Digger and Coffin Ed, antiheroic cultural agents, are damaged and deracinated by this systemic absurdity.

Absurdity is central to Himes's crime fiction precisely because the citizens of Harlem, including Coffin Ed and Grave Digger, have a contradictory relationship to white power structures. Bruce Franklin shrewdly places the logical absurdities of the antiheroes' dilemma in broad cultural perspective: "Himes's Black killer-detectives protect the people of Harlem by enforcing upon them the law and order of white capitalist America, doing this with a brutal and often literally blind violence their white colleagues can no longer employ with impunity, often committing more crimes than they solve. They embody what they represent, the ultimate stage of social disorder masquerading as order."[10] Crimes committed in Harlem therefore are not exclusively temporal but mythic. For Himes, only a radical social vision combined with grotesque artistic technique could illuminate the problematics of ideology in a world governed by capital.

The sense of evil pervading Himes's Harlem universe arises typically from the pursuit of money—that archetypal incarnation of capitalist values. The clear absence of honest capital in Harlem activates the absurd pursuit of money in any form by Himes's dedicated villains, who would simply imitate their more sedate white counterparts in the pursuit. Clearly the dividing line in this Harlem universe is between the select and corrupt haves and the disenfranchised mass of have-nots. Ideological conflict, expressed in the absurdist action writing Himes perfected, occurs across this line or chasm separating the poor, a sprawling lumpenproletariat, and the amoral criminal rich, who attain their financial advantage or power through a series of ruses, thefts, con games, and deceptions.

This frantic pursuit of money so central to bourgeois ethics can be traced in many of Himes's detective plots. In *For Love of Imabelle,* several preposterous scams—including the classic raising of money by turning ten-dollar into hundred-dollar bills, and the selling of fraudulent gold stock, as well as the search for a trunk of gold (which turns out to be fool's gold)—animate the action. In *The Heat's On,* pursuit by contesting criminals and various law enforcement agents of a lost heroin shipment worth $3 million results in outrageous, grotesque parody of the spirit of capitalism. Similarly, a bale of cotton containing $87,000 misappropriated from Harlem residents by Reverend Deke O'Malley in a phony back-to-Africa scheme triggers the conflict in *Cotton Comes to Harlem.* In *The Big Gold Dream,* the very title suggests the omnipotence of money—in this case, a maid's substantial numbers winnings and the criminal pursuit of it—that dictates the savage action. In *All Shot Up,* eight lives are extinguished for $50,000 in political payoff money. Within a culture ruled by such materialist pursuits, the ludicrous spirit of capitalism manifests itself in the frenetic, violent, criminal pursuit of money.

If mock capitalist intrigue is the source of the essential conflict between good and evil in Himes's Harlem crime fiction, the author seems more intent on exploring the absurdist implications of this phenomenon than in lodging a protest about it in the spirit of Richard Wright. "I wasn't showing the Negro as an oppressed, downtrodden people," he states in *My Life of Absurdity,* "but simply as an absurdity" (173). Creating almost implausibly grotesque action in an equally absurd world, Himes turned time and again to a rereading of Faulkner—specifically *Sanctuary* and *Light in August*—to sustain the harrowing comedy of his crime fiction. "I could lift scenes straight out of Faulkner and put them down in Harlem and all I had to change was the scene" (169). Faulkner, Himes's "secret mentor," suggests the extent to which Himes was shifting the boundaries of the world of detective fiction, bringing into focus through a range of comic devices a world in which evil and anarchy can scarcely be restrained.

Traditional crime fiction posits an essential chaos at the root of culture and then, if only cynically, reasserts forms of poetic justice; Himes focuses persistently on the divorce, as Camus would have it in *The Myth of Sisyphus,* between any unifying principle of justice and the irrational and meaningless nature of existence. Even when Grave Digger and Coffin Ed succeed in rescuing culture temporarily from chaos, they still see the world and themselves as fantastical and absurd. As black detectives upholding justice in Harlem, they apprehend that they are parodies of their white counterparts and are exceedingly self-conscious about their ambiguous roles. So consumed by violence and existential restlessness, they rarely retreat to their families and homes in Queens; indeed they rarely sleep. They are the yin and yang of violent retribution, oversized twins of mayhem who slap, beat, and shoot their way through Harlem, continually engaged in an archetypal chase.

Himes in *The Real Cool Killers,* a tightly plotted thriller, the second in the series, in which Coffin Ed and Grave Digger have to discover who killed a sadistic white man, Galen, who frequented Harlem bars in search of teenage girls, describes his two detectives in terms that would become ready-made for subsequent novels: "The two tall, lanky, loose-jointed detectives hit the pavement in unison, their nickel-plated .38 specials gripped in their hands. They looked like big-shouldered plowhands in Sunday suits at a Saturday night jamboree."[11] They are distinguished from each other only by Coffin Ed's horribly disfigured face, the result of an acid attack by hoodlums in *For Love of Imabelle.* Deriving partially from two middle-aged detectives in a story, "He Knew," that Himes had published in 1933 in *Abbott's Monthly Magazine,* they are most fully described in *All Shot Up:*[12]

Coffin Ed's hair was peppered with gray. He had a crescent-shaped scar on the right-side top of his skull, where Grave Digger had hit him with his pistol barrel, the time he had gone berserk after being blinded by acid thrown in his face. That had been more than three years ago, and the acid scars had been covered by skin grafted from his thigh. But the new skin was a shade or so lighter than his natural face skin and it had been grafted on in pieces. The result was that Coffin Ed's face looked as though it had been made up in Hollywood for the role of the

Frankenstein monster. Grave Digger's rough, lumpy face could have belonged to
any number of hard, Harlem characters.[13]

Operating out of the 116th Street precinct under the apprehensive but understanding eye of their white superior, Lieutenant Anderson, these two detectives, whose very names symbolize death, are the apostles and explicators
of the absurd inner world of Harlem violence.

Unlike most of their detective predecessors, Coffin Ed and Grave Digger
are legendary figures in their community. They instill respect and a certain
amount of terror in the populace. In *For Love of Imabelle,* Himes writes in his
typically laconic style that "folks in Harlem believed that Grave Digger Jones
and Coffin Ed Johnson would shoot a man stone dead for not standing in a
straight line" (52). Local humor also permeates another legend in *All Shot
Up:* "The story was in Harlem that these two black detectives would kill a
dead man in his coffin if he so much as moved" (30). They are defined existentially by their paradoxical roles. Grave Digger, somewhat more philosophical than his companion, relishes the thought that a killing in Harlem, as
he expresses it in *The Real Cool Killers,* is "the greatest show on earth" (151).
Yet in the same novel, Grave Digger senses their limitations: "This is Harlem.
Nobody knows all the connections here" (44). Both detectives push at the
limits of meaning, experiencing the exhilaration and terror of the absurd.
Antiheroes centered in Himes's antigenre, they are fantastical, Herculean figures, native sons struggling with sensational and peculiarly indigenous forms
of American violence in an effort to protect their culture from chaos.

Gallery of Grotesques

Seen through the distorting lens of the absurd, the characters in Himes's
detective novels often seem like comic monsters at a masked ball. Julian
Symons, in his historical study of crime fiction, states, "The humans among
whom the detectives move are credulous, lecherous, treacherous, greedy and
savage."[14] In Himes's fiction, they are monstrously grotesque in their outlines, tending toward caricature—metaphorical extensions of a desolate and
depleted human landscape.

Himes had a rare talent for populating his demonic world with grotesques. These deformed figures, who constitute a gallery of absurd humanity, help to explain Himes's radical social vision, for their exaggerated
deformities are emblems of the absence of orderly arrangement in the culture
they inhabit and prey upon. Himes began to populate his world with grotesques in his first Harlem crime novel, *For Love of Imabelle.* The protagonist,

a young man named Jackson, steals money from his employer, the celebrated Harlem undertaker H. Exodus Clay, who appears in several of the Harlem novels. Jackson also is in love with Imabelle, who has stolen a trunk of fool's gold from her husband, a con artist who is a member of a vicious three-man gang that has been selling false gold stock to black people across America.

Jackson has a twin brother, Goldy, who impersonates a nun named "Sister Gabriel" and lives with two other female impersonators, Big Kathy and Lady Gypsy, the triumvirate known collectively as "The Three Black Widows." (Tricks and disguises, linked to the criminals' attempting to outwit criminals, is a common motif in the Harlem novels.) When Goldy involves himself in the search for the gold, a member of the gang cuts his throat and stuffs him in Clay's 1947 Cadillac hearse. Crammed in the hearse with other paraphernalia, Goldy projects an end that is grim, grotesque, and wild:

Underneath the trunk black cloth was piled high. Artificial flowers were scattered about in garish disarray. A horseshoe wreath of artificial lilies had slipped to the back. Looking out from the arch of white lilies was a blackface. The face was looking backward from a head-down position, resting on the back of the skull. A white bonnet sat atop a grey wig which had fallen askew. The face was a horrible grimace of pure evil. White-walled eyes stared at the four gray men with a fixed, unblinking stare. Beneath the face was the huge purple-lipped wound of a cut throat. (149)

Pandemonium erupts as Jackson drives the runaway hearse through the stalls of the Harlem market, with both his brother's corpse and the trunk of ore toppling out. Following another round of grotesque violence in which two members of the gang are killed, order is restored, with Jackson getting both his old job back and his girl, Imabelle. Grave Digger and Coffin Ed, somewhat peripheral figures, seem almost overwhelmed by the terrifying absurdity of the situation, and indeed Grave Digger, disoriented by the acid attack on his partner, is left "riding the crest of a rage" (189) as he attempts to square justice with a persistently chaotic and paradoxical situation.

Himes's predilection for grotesque caricature continues at the outside of his second crime novel, *The Crazy Kill*. Originally entitled *A Jealous Man Can't Win* and in French *Couché dans le pain*, Himes began the novel in January 1957 after rereading Faulkner's *Sanctuary;* he finished it 1 May. He based the novel on a café tale told by his friend the cartoonist Ollie Harrington "about a man falling out of a window in Harlem in the early hours of morning during a wake, and landing unhurt in a basket of bread. . . . It was a simple domestic story which involved a couple of killings and my two detectives, Grave Digger and Coffin Ed" (*My Life of Absurdity*, 120).

Himes begins with multiple plot threads and grotesque mystification as the Reverend Short, presiding over the wake of a famous Harlem gambler, Big Joe Pullen, leans too far out of the third floor window while observing a man stealing a bag of money from the automobile of an A&P manager and plummets into a loaf of bread. The Reverend, a "short squat midget" with a fondness for drug-laced alcohol, falls in cinematic slow motion: "Slowly his hips leaned out. His buttocks rose into the light like a slow-rolling wave, then dropped below the window ledge as his legs and feet slowly rose into the air. For a long moment the silhouette of two feet sitting upside down on top of two legs was suspended in the yellow-lighted rectangle. Then it sank slowly from view, like a body going head-down into water."[15] Reverend Short's fortunate fall or benign immersion in bread invites a comic contradiction that rapidly turns sinister, for shortly after he picks himself up from the "mattress of soft bread" and returns to the wake, another body, that of Valentine Haines, is found stabbed to death on the same soft, mortal bed.

As it turns out, the famous gambler whom Haines worked for, Johnny Perry, is as responsible for solving the crime as are Grave Digger and Coffin Ed—another involuted technique that Himes employs in his experimental detective fiction. In fact, Grave Digger serves as a worldly philosopher framing Johnny's own efforts at detection. At one point, Grave Digger observes, "This is Harlem. . . . Ain't no other place like it in the world. You've got to start from scratch here, because these folks in Harlem do things for reasons nobody else in the world would think of" (56). Starting from scratch, Johnny undertakes "to straighten out some of these mysteries" (134). His inquiries parallel those of the two detectives. Ultimately it is the deranged grotesque, Reverend Short, a holy roller whose nearsighted eyes are described as "bulging like bananas being squeezed from thinskins" (78), who is uncovered as the murderer, largely out of perverse passion for Dulcey, Johnny's mildly licentious, highly manipulative wife.

Johnny himself is smart, tough, dignified, even generous as he throws change to the kids of Harlem, but he too is lethal. Himes's description of the gambler also shows the destructive element implicit in the grotesque: "In the center of his forehead was a puffed, bluish scar with ridges pronging off like immobilized octopus tentacles. It gave him an expression of perpetual rage, which was accentuated by the smoldering fire that lay always just beneath the surface of his muddy brown eyes, ready to flame into a blaze" (29). While Coffin Ed and Grave Digger ultimately arrest Reverend Short, Johnny must kill Chink Charley, who had been trying to blackmail Dulcey for $10,000. It is implied that his lawyer will extricate him from any criminal charge. Johnny, his humane impulses thwarted by jealousy for Dulcey, nevertheless mediates his way, as do Grave Digger and Coffin Ed, through a grotesque universe where the craziest of kills never conform to normal distinctions and expectations.

By the time he started his third crime novel, *The Real Cool Killers,* whose original title was *If Trouble Was Money* and in French *Il pleu des coups durs,* Himes had perfected a grotesque descriptive technique that ranged broadly from the playful to the most sinister and terrifying and embraced both central and peripheral characters. Often even the peripheral grotesques are central to the action in ways that are only slowly apprehended by both the reader and Himes's two detectives. Thus, at the outset of *The Real Cool Killers,* a small, aging black man at Harlem's Dew Drop Inn accosts a white soda salesman, Ulysses Galen, with a knife, forcing the bartender to lop off the black man's arm with an axe: "The severed arm in its coat sleeve, still clutching the knife, sailed through the air, sprinkling the nearby spectators with drops of blood, landed on the linoleum floor, and skidded beneath the table of a booth" (8). The elderly assailant, who has accused the white man of "diddling my little girls," searches frantically for his severed arm in order to continue the fight, before fainting from loss of blood. The white man, in turn, upon leaving the bar is chased down 127th Street in a Keystone Cops scene involving dozens of Harlem's citizenry, a "grotesque silhouette" who ultimately is killed. The little black man was onto a "crime" perpetrated by Galen—the procurement of young women for sadistic sexual purposes—which Coffin Ed and Grave Digger will learn about only slowly. As for Galen, his true murderer remains undetected almost until the end of this bizarre narrative.

Contributing to the ominous and fantastic world of this novel is the presence of a teenage gang, the Real Cool Moslems. Himes was almost prescient in sensing, in the late 1950s, the emergence of the Black Muslim movement as a force in Harlem life and typically cynical in his treatment of this phenomenon. Early in the novel, the eight "real cool" Moslems taunt Coffin Ed and Grave Digger, with lethal results:

"Praise Allah," the tallest of the Arabs said.

As though performing a ritual, the others said, "Mecca," and all bowed low with outstretched arms.

"Cut the comedy and straighten up," Grave Digger said. "We're holding you as witnesses."

"Who's got the prayer?" the leader asked with bowed head.

"I've got the prayer," another replied.

"Pray to the great monster," the leader commanded.

The one who had the prayer turned slowly and presented his white-robed back-side to Coffin Ed. A sound like a hound dog baying issued from his rear end. (19)

Compounding this flatulent insult, another Arab attempts to sprinkle sacred scented holy water on Coffin Ed, who, mistaking it for acid, shoots him dead. Within the early chapters of *The Real Cool Killers,* a gallery of grotesques bent on careless but murderous "fun" creates a world that breaks apart for the two detectives. Coffin Ed is suspended, and Grave Digger, like "a dangerous animal escaped from the zoo" (66), rages through Harlem, "solving" the crime and even discovering that Ed's daughter, Sugartit, had been involved with the Moslems and almost with Galen. Gravedigger figures correctly that Sissie, another gang member, had killed Galen in order to protect Sugartit, and although the power structure decides to bury this information, Grave Digger and Coffin Ed have gone mildly berserk, killing off Moslems in order to rescue Ed's daughter. Despite an anticlimactic resolution restoring order, the dominant impression in the novel is one of mounting emotional and mental disorientation, a "macabre pantomime" (35) involving dangerous rogues bent on driving Coffin Ed and Grave Digger deeper into hell.

Adding to this dissolution into a grotesque state of being is Himes's penchant for splitting the action and scenes within a simultaneous time frame so that sequences of the conflict parallel and confound each other. For example, in chapter 9, Digger visits a whorehouse seeking information, while in chapters 8 and 10 the police are checking an apartment inhabited by the Moslems. A standard narrative technique in Himes's crime fiction, this tracking of the conflict tends to heighten Digger and Coffin Ed's disorientation by leaving them partially in the dark and continually subject to the vagaries of grotesque existence.

The crimes committed by Himes's early rogues and villains render them grotesque and also force Coffin Ed and Grave Digger to contend with their absurdly violent behavior. Such comic villains, however, do not inspire the sort of dread that hovers over Himes's fourth crime novel, *Run Man Run* (1966), originally published by Gallimard in 1959 as *Dare-Dare.* The harrowing power of darkness in this novel comes not from black criminals operating beyond the fringes of the law but rather from a white murderer—a police detective—operating within the establishment. Matt Walker is the archetypal white murderer run amok, and Himes's perspective on him and his main quarry, an educated black man named Jimmy who has witnessed Walker's senseless murder of two fellow porters at a midtown automat, is unique. (Himes had worked temporarily at a Horn and Hardart automat restaurant in New York in 1955 in order to earn money for passage back to Paris.)

Himes uses the mazes and passages under midtown Manhattan as a counterpoint to Walker's monomaniacal search for Jimmy Johnson, first at the scene of the crime and then through Harlem. Walker is the emblem of grotesque evil, forcing awareness of a racist culture on Jimmy. He is sadistic and amoral, operating in a "maniacal trance," killing black people dispassionately. Himes reveals Walker's absurd destructiveness in the shooting of a porter, Fat Sam: "He fell forward, pulling the tray from the rack along with him. Thick, cold, three-day old turkey gravy poured over his kinky head as he landed, curled up like a fetus, between a five-gallon can of whipping cream and the wooden crate of iceberg lettuce" (17). Walker is both mad and nihilistic. The anarchic blindness of his violent behavior cannot be checked by a suitably armed Johnson but only by his brother-in-law, a cop named Brock, who shoots Walker dead at the end of the novel. Walker is not, however, seriocomic. He is pure demonism, pure dread, turning the world grotesque for Jimmy.

With *The Big Gold Dream,* Himes retreats from his savage critique of white power structures to a more characteristic satire on the religious dimension of Harlem life. Here, Himes's gallery of grotesques typically includes preachers, fanatics, and born-again converts who prey on each other and the community. In *The Big Gold Dream,* the grotesque Sweet Prophet Brown ministers to the "black, brown and yellow people" of Harlem. He is a fantastic con artist, a "fabulous" man who can mesmerize thousands. At his revival meetings on Harlem's streets, he exchanges sacred bread crumbs for one-to twenty-dollar donations from each convert. Himes describes Sweet Prophet in bizarre terms: "His tremendous bulk was impressive in a bright purple robe lined with yellow silk and trimmed with mink. Beneath it he wore a black taffeta suit with white piping and silver buttons. His fingernails, untrimmed since he first claimed to have spoken with God, were more than three inches in length. They curled like strange talons, and were painted different colors. On each finger he wore a diamond ring. His smooth black face with its buck teeth and popping eyes was ageless; but his long grizzly hair, on which he wore a black silk cap, was snow-white."[16] The Prophet, who believes that "faith is a big gold dream," is like "a carnival on the loose" (86). His obsession with money—"It takes a lot of money to be a prophet these days. It's the high cost of living" (204)—is an index to the similar fixations of his congregation, as well as the strictly secular representatives of the Harlem community, who will kill for their own big gold dream. Moreover, as with Johnny in *The Real Cool Killers,* the Prophet shrewdly takes the pulse of the

Harlem community, figuring out who had stolen numbers winnings from one of his parishioners (and taking the $36,000 from her in turn) before Coffin Ed and Digger arrive at a similar discovery.

Apocalypse

By 1959, as Himes began *All Shot Up,* he admitted that he "was having great difficulty keeping [his] detective stories absurd" (*My Life of Absurdity,* 196). He was now "the most celebrated writer in France who couldn't speak French" (199), and also the most famous "Série noire" writer. With the Algerian War at its greatest intensity and serving perhaps as a subliminal impulse, Himes in *All Shot Up* turned to the political arena to fashion another mayhem novel in which absurdly violent action claims eight lives. Here Himes's obsession with sex, violence, and political depravity can scarcely be contained within a complex comic structure. His primary world is now unredeemably evil and apocalyptic in its grotesque outlines, more profoundly sinister than in his earlier crime fiction.

One of the early victims is a transvestite pimp named Black Beauty, who is hit so violently by thieves driving a gold Cadillac that he is hurled through the air and crucified against a wall of a convent: "They discovered an iron bar protruding from the wall at a point about six feet high. Below and above it there were deep cracks in the cement; and, at one point above, the crack had been dug out to form a long, oblong hole. The face of the corpse had been thrust into this hole with sufficient force to clamp it, and the end of the bar was caught between the legs, holding it aloft" (41). However comical this tableau might be, the comedy is overwhelmed by a sense of violent transgression. In fact, as Coffin Ed and Digger begin to investigate the merging worlds of homosexual and political manipulation (Himes's homophobia and essentially negative political anarchism fuel his vision), they find the early deaths that animate *All Shot Up* a special order of viciousness.

Within the sexual and political superstructure of evil dominating *All Shot Up,* most forms of violence are bizarre. In one tour de force of grotesque mayhem, the thief, who is attempting to escape from Digger and Coffin Ed, is decapitated by sheets of steel protruding from a truck:

The three thin sheets of stainless steel, six feet in width, with red flags flying from both corners, formed a blade less than a quarter of an inch thick. This blade caught the rider above his woolen-lined jacket, on the exposed part of his neck, which was stretched and taut from his physical exertion, as the motorcycle went underneath. He was hitting more than fifty-five miles an hour, and the blade severed his head from his body as though he had been guillotined.

The truck driver glanced from his window to watch the passing truck as he kept braking to a stop. But instead he saw a man without a head passing on a motorcycle with a sidecar and a stream of steaming red blood flowing back in the wind.

He gasped and passed out.

His lax feet released the pressure from the brake and clutch, and the truck kept on ahead.

The motorcycle, ridden by a man without a head, surged forward at a rapid clip. . . .

The truck carrying the sheet metal turned gradually to the right from faulty steering mechanism. It climbed over the shallow curb and started up the wide stone steps of a big fashionable Negro church.

In the lighted box out in front of the church was the announcement of the sermon for the day.

Beware! Death is closer than you think!

The head rolled off the slow-moving truck, dropped to the sidewalk and rolled out into the street. Grave Digger, closing up fast, saw something that looked like a football with a cap on it bouncing on the black asphalt. It was caught in his one bright light, but the top was turned to him when he saw it, and he didn't recognize what it was.

"What did he throw out?" he asked Coffin Ed.

Coffin Ed was staring as though petrified. He gulped. "His head," he said.

After digressing into an account of the two detectives' problems when a truck hits them from behind, Himes returns to conclude his account of the headless motorcyclist:

Gradually the taut headless body on the motorcycle spewed out its blood and the muscles went limp. The motorcycle began to waver; it went to one side and then the other, crossed 125th Street, just missing a taxi, neatly circled around the big clock atop a post at the corner and crashed into the iron-barred door of the credit jewelry store, knocking down a sign that read:

We Will Give Credit to the Dead. (84–85)

This passage is an extraordinary evocation of the apocalyptic drama that has been building in Himes's detective fiction. The frantic narrative pace, grotesque description, terse irony, and pungent dialogue are concomitants of the jumbled and disintegrative world that Coffin Ed and Grave Digger hustle through. Such an extravagant style gives rise to the creation of grotesque characters and a grotesque landscape. In this tableau, the disparate elements of comedy and horror brought together at the point of violent death are the penultimate frame for Himes's evolving vision of an absurd, malignant, apocalyptic world.

Perhaps Himes never felt comfortable with the affirmative vision that underpins the successful solution of crimes in detective fiction, for he consciously parodies the genre from the outset and progressively explodes it with apocalyptic delight. Thus the violent deaths in Himes's infernal novel *The Heat's On,* running to twelve (with additional beatings and maimings), exceeds even the relentless killings in *All Shot Up.* From the outset of *The Heat's On,* first published in 1961 by Gallimard as *Ne nous enverons pas,* Coffin Ed and Digger are in a labyrinth of enigmatic violence. A monstrous, idiotic giant, Pinky, whom Himes's describes as "a milk-white albino with pinkeyes, battered lips, cauliflowered ears and thick, Kinky, cream-colored hair" (7), has put in a false fire alarm at Riverside Church in order to alert detectives not to a fire but to a conflagration of another order—the robbery and murder of his father, Gus, by an African and his step-mother. As the two detectives begin to check out Pinky's story (Gus's body, stuffed in a truck, is not found until the end of the novel), they do so with a bizarre sense of impending apocalypse. Ed observes, "It'd be a hell of a note if somebody was being murdered during all the comedy we're having," to which Digger replies in laconic hermeneutic code, "That would be the story" (20). The comedy the detectives allude to is the fruitless attempt by squads of police and firefighters to beat and shoot Pinky into submission for having called in the false fire alarm. Yet his alarm is an ironic prefiguration of the catastrophes awaiting people, including Ed and Digger, in the novel.

As is typical of Himes's other crime fiction, the logical-temporal realm of *The Heat's On* is explosively compressed. The action begins at 1:20 A.M. on a viciously hot Harlem summer night and concludes with Aristotelian intensity the same day. Thus the virtual hecatomb of bloodletting that spills from this constricted time frame seems to feed inversely on the very framework of detective fiction. In a brilliant study of detective fiction, Dennis Porter observes that "it is a genre committed to the act of recovery, moving forward in order to move back. The detective encounters effects without causes, events in jumbled chronological order, significant clues hidden among the insignificant. And his role is to reestablish sequence and causality."[17] Yet the sheer magnitude of the murders in *The Heat's On,* these multiple crimes against the community, seem to parody the ability of Himes's detectives to restore order through discovery.

As the novel unfolds, the apocalyptic element is scarcely contained. Ed and Grave Digger have to break up a half-dozen fights along Seventh Avenue before getting back to their precinct. Later, at 5:27 A.M. (Himes fixes action at precise times and then shatters this mosaic by creating overlapping temporal frames involving other characters), they stop for gumbo at a nightclub on 125th Street, where "the tight close air was churned to a steaming bedlam" (37). By early morning they are charged with unwarranted brutality in the death of Jake Kubansky, a dwarf who had been arguing with Pinky at the outset of the novel. Jake had been a drug pusher, and Digger had punched him once in the stomach, exploding pouches of narcotics that he had swallowed to avoid detection. Observes Digger of their suspension by the commissioner, "It's all right to kill a few colored people for trying to get their children an education, but don't hurt a mother-raping white punk for selling dope" (68). Himes's allusion to the civil rights movement compounds the ambiguities the two detectives perceive as they try to "make a decent peaceful city for people to live in" (220).

Harlem, however, diverges radically in *The Heat's On* from any image of a peaceful city. Crime provides the dramatic tension as criminals and police frantically pursue heroin worth $3 million that Gus had hidden. Even the law of entropy seems to govern the apocalyptic landscape. For instance, in one remarkable scene, the house of the grotesque Sister Heavenly, an aged but lethal faith healer who is Pinky's aunt, is inadvertently blown up with nitroglycerin by her faithful employee Uncle Heavenly, who has been trying to pick her safe:

Strangely enough, the house disintegrated in only three directions—forward, backward and upward. The front went out across the street, and such items as the bed, tables, chest of drawers and a handpainted enamel chamber pot crashed into the front of the neighbor's house. Sister Heavenly's clothes, some of which dated back to the 1920's were strewn over the street like a weird coverlet of many colors. The back of the house, along with the kitchen stove, refrigerator, table and chairs, Uncle Saint's bunk and lockbox, crockery and kitchen utensils, went over the back fence into the vacant lot. . . . While the top of the house, attic included, along with the old upright piano, Sister Heavenly's throne and souvenir trunk, sailed straight up into the air, and long after the sound of the blast had died away the piano could be heard playing up there all alone. . . .

But the floor of the house remained intact. It had been swept clean of every loose scrap, every pin and needle, every particle of dust, but the smooth surface of the wood and linoleum went undamaged. (116–17)

The world that Himes incarnates in grotesque description and action in this novel moves irrevocably toward extinction. Even the final irony has an apocalyptic resonance, for the cretin, Pinky, admits that he has thrown three eel skins stuffed with the heroin into an incinerator and burned the object of so much pursuit.

Himes modulates the violence in his next novel, *Cotton Comes to Harlem*, in which he achieves fine formal control in adjusting the apocalyptic element to a vision of social manipulation and disintegration. Published initially by Plon in 1964 as *Retour en Afrique* and in English by Putnam's in 1965, *Cotton Comes to Harlem* fixes on the back-to-Africa movement popularized initially by Marcus Garvey and in the 1960s by the black power movement. Himes stated in his interview with John Williams that he wrote *Cotton Comes to Harlem* in order to expose the absurdity of contemporary back-to-Africa movements. "It probably didn't make sense even then, but it's even *less* logical now, because the black people of America aren't Africans anymore, and the Africans don't want them."[18] Himes in the novel parodies the millenarian promise of the Reverend Deke O'Malley, a "Communist Christian" preacher who steals $87,000 from eighty-seven Harlem families, as well as the home-styled promise of Colonel Robert L. Calhoun's "back-to-the-South" crusade. Caught between perverted white and black dialectics of deception, the people of Harlem find themselves in a demonic rather than a promised land. *Cotton Comes to Harlem*, which was released as a film in 1970, is notably successful in Himes's detective series because of its satiric portrait of white and black tricksters' preying on people's lost dreams.

The opening sequence once again hurls the reader into a perilously grotesque and contradictory world where pandemonium rules. Deke's barbecue and rally to boost his back-to-Africa movement, which takes in $87,000, is in turn held up violently by southern-styled white men who escape in a meat truck; these con artists are pursued in turn by Deke and his bodyguards in a hail of machine-gun bullets. The death of one of Deke's recruiters reveals Himes's genius for bizarre description: "There was a burst from a machine gun. A mixture of teeth, barbecued pork ribs, and human brains flew through the air like macabre birds" (13). The tense stylistic virtuosity of Himes's clashing images and metaphors suggests his maturing ability to evoke a comic volcano as the essence of Harlem life.

In this novel, Grave Digger returns to his Harlem beat after six months of recuperation from his near-fatal shooting by Benny Mason's men in *The Heat's On*. Both Digger and Coffin Ed continue to resemble, to their superior Lieutenant Anderson, "two hog farmers on a weekend in the Big Town" (18). Anderson, trying to subdue the apocalyptic element in Harlem life, wants the two detectives to reduce their brutality in their handling of the crime. The apoplectic Digger responds: "We got the highest crime rate on earth among the colored people in Harlem. And there ain't but three things to do about it:

Make the criminals pay for it—you don't want to do that; pay the people enough to live decently—you ain't going to do that; so all that's left is let 'em eat one another up" (20). Digger's philosophical ruminations are inherently nihilistic at this point in Himes's Harlem cycle.

Even Anderson senses that this world is breaking apart. As he leafs through the day's reports, Digger and Ed provide tersely grotesque glosses on the contents:

"Man kills his wife with an ax for burning his breakfast pork chop . . . man shoots another man demonstrating a recent shooting he had witnesses . . . man stabs another man for spilling beer on his new suit . . . man kills self in a bar playing Russian roulette with a .32 revolver . . . woman stabs man in stomach fourteen times, no reason given . . . woman scalds neighboring woman with pot of boiling water for speaking to her husband . . . man arrested for threatening to blow up subway train because he entered wrong station and couldn't get his token back—"

"All colored citizens," Coffin Ed interrupted.

Anderson ignored it. "Man sees stranger wearing his own new suit, slashes him with a razor," he read on. "Man dressed as Cherokee Indian splits white bartender's skull with homemade tomahawk . . . man arrested on Seventh Avenue for hunting cats with hound dog and shotgun . . . twenty-five men arrested for trying to chase all the white people out of Harlem—"

"It's Independence Day," Grave Digger interrupted. (20–21)

The mounting metaphysical disorientation that everyone senses on this sweltering Fourth of July guarantees more violent disruptions. One reviewer of Himes's detective fiction observes, "Against such a landscape, the violent opening of each novel constitutes less a crime to be solved than an overture promising more mayhem to come."[19] In fact, Digger and Ed, assigned to protect Deke, now an informer, try as much to subdue the grotesque as they do solve crimes. What they bring to the light in *Cotton Comes to Harlem* is the chaotic absurdity at the center of peoples' crazed pursuit of a single bale of stolen cotton containing Deke's criminal spoils.

The universe of *Cotton Comes to Harlem* is one of total deception. Deke, for instance, both is and is not what he seems, utilizing his multiple disguises to outwit unsuspecting Harlem residents, stay ahead of the Syndicate out to kill him, elude the police, and seduce women. Digger and Ed manage to apprehend him, but they still know that they are "missing something." As Himes cuts and shifts the action, they cannot unmask all of the ludicrous deceptions keeping them from the bale of cotton.

At the end of the novel, the grotesque *auto-de-fé* in Deke's church as the detective's tracer bullets literally ignite two thugs is symptomatic of the uncanny apocalyptic element that persistently erupts in Himes's later detective fiction. Digger shoots one criminal in the leg, watching it "break off like a wooden stick" and the trousers catch on fire. Two more bullets set the howling thief totally aflame. "The dying man clawed at the book rack above him, breaking the fragile wood, and a prayer book fell on top of his burning body" (202). Digger and Ed then turn to the second thief and systematically pump bullets into him, igniting him until he slumps "across the bench in a kneeling posture, as though praying in fire" (203). By now, the church is an apocalyptic inferno: "Now the entire platform holding the pulpit and the choir and the organ was burning brightly, lighting up the stained-glass pictures of the saints looking down from the windows. From outside came a banshee wail as the first of the cruisers came tearing down the street" (203). Fire, carnage, and inhuman sounds combine to transform Deke's church into an infernal realm rendered alien by the rush of events.

The apocalyptic sphere of violence of *Cotton Comes to Harlem* dissipates only when Ed and Digger capture the colonel and demand $87,000 from him to return to Harlem's conjured families. The original $87,000 had been discovered by the junkman, Uncle Bud, who presciently had gone back to Africa, where he bought 500 cattle and exchanged them for 100 wives. The parodic element comes full circle but not before a sinister world has been erected and destroyed by Himes.

Chester Himes's last novel in his Harlem crime cycle, *Blind Man with a Pistol,* confirms his preoccupation with an apocalyptic universe while playing havoc with conventional expectations of the detective genre. Himes began the novel in Holland in 1967 after hearing the true story of a blind man with a pistol shooting up Brooklyn from his guest, Phil Lomax. Himes in *My Life of Absurdity* confesses that the story signalled something to him, forcing him back to the beginnings of his earlier detective stories: "It worried me because it was telling me something" (347). At the same time, Himes was enjoying international celebrity status and relative affluence from film options on his detective fiction, following Samuel Goldwyn, Jr.'s., decision to adapt *Cotton Comes to Harlem.* Nevertheless he delayed traveling to Hollywood and concentrated on *Blind Man with a Pistol,* which he acknowledges "was not a customary type of detective story" (348). Himes's agent, Roslyn Targ, found the manuscript "wild, bawdy, shocking and very exciting" (350), selling it to William Morrow. What so gripped Himes as he wrote his last novel was his apprehension that any solution to "crime" in Harlem remains inaccessible, for Coffin Ed and Grave Digger in their final appearance preside over a highly politicized world that breaks apart.

At the outset of *Blind Man with a Pistol,* Himes immediately destroys any conventional expectations readers might have of detective fiction by providing not one but three forewords and a bawdy poem, each revealing the absurdities of the Harlem condition. One concise anecdotal prologue captures the grin lurking behind Himes's murderous universe:

> "Blink once, you're robbed," Coffin Ed advised the white man slumming in Harlem.
> "Blink twice, you're dead," Grave Digger added drily. (*Blind Man with a Pistol*)

Indeed actions and events are so swift and disjointed in the novel that characters—notably the two detectives—find themselves on a grotesque rollercoaster. Demonic forces are operative in this universe that wit and satire can scarcely contain.

The world of *Blind Man with a Pistol* is totally estranged from human and social norms. Action begins at a dilapidated three-story brick house on 119th Street that is the church site of Reverend Sam (who claims to be one hundred years old), his eleven Mormon wives, and teeming progeny. Sam is the embodiment of human grotesquerie: "He was clean shaven, and his sagging parchment-like skin which seemed but a covering for his skeleton was tight about his face like a leather mask. Wrinkled lids, looking more like dried skin, drooped over his milky bluish eyes, giving him a vague similarity to an old snapping turtle" (18–19). The squalor that surrounds the reverend and his tribe is a surrealist metaphor for the chaotic, collapsed world of Harlem. Reverend Sam's fifty naked children, for example, assume subhuman shape as they settle in for lunch, observed by police from the Harlem precinct who have been called to the tenement by a sign hanging outside advertising for a fertile woman: "At the time of their arrival the children were having lunch, which consisted of the stewed pigsfeet and chitterlings which Bubber, the cretin, had been cooking in the washing pot. It had been divided equally and poured into three rows of troughs in the middle room on the first floor. The naked children were lined up, side by side, on hands and knees, swilling it like pigs" (21). Both the banality and the heightened illusion of surreality that the scene projects contribute to Himes's immediate construction of a precarious world gone slightly mad.

Himes's reductionist and absurdist techniques in two initial chapters, which James Lundquist rightfully evaluates as "the strangest in American literature," are juxtaposed against the first "Interlude" or interchapter.[20] These interludes, which Himes spaces throughout the novel much in the collage-like fashion of John Dos Passos in his *U.S.A.* trilogy, move from a vision of an earlier, ordered world of Harlem existence to a grotesque and ambiguous world of appearances. Yet the first interlude—a geographic and historical tour of Harlem as the mecca for black people—is almost pristine in its normalcy. The author zooms in on the old Theresa Hotel where everyone from Booker T. Washington to Louis Armstrong stayed in the old days. Here is a version of urban pastoral that is poignant as it contrasts jarringly with the more dominant impression of the absence of order and meaning in *Blind Man with a Pistol*.

A great deal of the action occurs around the Theresa, located on 125th Street and Seventh Avenue, and if the splendor of the hotel was once a norm for the vitality of Harlem, Himes cunningly contrives apocalyptic episodes to reveal how far Harlem had deviated from the norm in the 1960s. Nowhere does contemporary history weigh more heavily on Himes's artistic consciousness than in this novel—an absurdist critique of a volatile American decade that the author largely was viewing from afar as an exile. The satiric power of Himes's apocalyptic vision obliterates the millennial hopes that characterized the 1960s. With cataclysmic glee he attacks communal life as typified by the Reverend Sam, interracial sex, gay liberation, black power, Black Jesus, the Black Muslims, an assortment of evangelical enterprises, civil rights, and integration. A great comic disaster lurks in virtually every chapter of this grotesque novel, a cataclysm that ultimately swallows the apostles of law and order, Grave Digger and Coffin Ed.

By the time that Coffin Ed and Digger appear in their dilapidated car in chapter 3, passing along "practically unseen, like a ghostly vehicle floating in the dark, its occupants invisible" (43), they are just trying to take it easy on a sweltering Harlem night. Already, however, a white homosexual has been killed by a black man wearing a fez, and Marcus Mackenzie, a new black Messiah preaching sexual brotherhood with his Nordic goddess Birgit, has started on an orgiastic march with his disciples:

When the marchers came abreast of the 125th Street station on upper Park Avenue, a long straggling tail of laughing, dancing, hysterical black and white people had attached itself to the original forty-eight. Black and white people came from the station waiting room to stare in popeyed amazement. Black and white people came from nearby bars, from the dim stinking doorways, from the flea bag hotels, from the cafeterias, the greasy spoons, from the shoe shine parlors, the poolrooms—pansies and prostitutes, ordinary bar drinkers and strangers in the area who had stopped for a bite to eat, Johns and squares looking for excitement, muggers and sneak thieves looking for victims. The scene that greeted them was like a carnival. It was a hot night. Some of them were drunk. Others had nothing to do. They joined the carnival group thinking maybe they were headed for a revival meeting, a sex orgy, a pansy ball, a beer festival, a baseball game. The white people attracted by the black. The black people attracted by the white. (41)

Surrounded by progressive sequences of grotesque action, the two detectives know that an easy time for them is ephemeral.

Solving the crime of the murdered white homosexual and a potentially related multiple murder and theft of a Gladstone bag filled with money from a quack, Dr. Mabuta, who poses as an African witch doctor promising eternal life through his youth elixir, is what interests Digger and Coffin Ed. Instead they are assigned to monitor and investigate numerous demonstrations and riots that are erupting in Harlem, for the outgoing precinct captain, Brice, sees a subversive pattern behind them. In fact, Captain Brice and Lieutenant Anderson do not want their two best detectives working on homicides—an ironic inversion of what they do best. Thus the detectives are diverted from the primary crime by a more tenuous criminal investigation of conspiracy. The bizarre rush of events and their new job description as political agents or detectives renders them incapable or blind before forces that they only dimly apprehend.

The motif of blindness framing the novel permits Himes to explore in comic fashion some major political and eschatological themes that had been building in his crime fiction for a decade. All of the radical disruptions of the 1960s center symbolically on Harlem in *Blind Man with a Pistol,* giving rise to a variety of prophets who would strip away the political blindness of the populace. Yet each prophet in turn parodies his apocalyptic vision by engaging in trickery and manipulation.

Marcus MacKenzie suffers from megalomania and a compulsive desire to be loved by white women. Dr. Mubuta is an avatar of Uncle Sam. His elixir—a grotesque concoction of baboon testicles, feathers, eyes, mating organs of rabbits, eagles, and shellfish—is designed to grant blacks extended life so that they can outlast the white race. Similarly, the black power advocate, Doctor Moore, is merely a pimp who provides high-priced prostitutes to a white clientele at the Americana Hotel. And then there is the ludicrous General Ham, a fake prophet who would draft Christ for the cause of black militancy, turning Him into a revolutionary Black Jesus in order to destroy the white race. Yet even as Himes satirizes the various messianic crusades of the 1960s, he continues to probe those political mysteries that define historically the nature of power and powerlessness in contemporary America.

Even the two detectives are subjected to Himes's satirical point of view. Toward the middle of the novel, unable to function as they once did, they must scrutinize the absurdity of their earthly condition:

The two black detectives looked at one another. Their short-cropped hair was salted with gray and they were thicker around their middles. Their faces bore the lumps and

scars they had collected in the enforcement of law in Harlem. Now after twelve years
as first grade precinct detectives they hadn't been promoted. Their raises in salaries
hadn't kept up with the rise of the cost of living. They hadn't finished paying for
their houses. Their private cars had been bought on credit. And yet they hadn't taken
a dime in bribes. Their entire career as cops had been one long period of turmoil.
When they weren't taking lumps from the thugs, they were taking lumps from the
commissioners. Now they were curtailed in their own duties. And they didn't expect
it to change. (24–25)

Grave Digger and Coffin Ed are anachronisms in the 1960s, superannu-
ated cops overwhelmed by political and medical disruptions. Crime is
now a pretext permitting Himes to explore comically his vision of an
urban apocalypse.

Digger and Coffin Ed, deflected from their primary quest, cannot hope to
cover the twists and turns unfolding on Nat Turner Day in Harlem. Himes
brings the disparate strands of action together in a controlling design as various marching factions converge on Seventh Avenue and 125th Street in chapter 12: "It was all really funny, in a grotesque way. The lynched black Jesus
who looked like a runaway slave. The slick-looking young man with his for-
eign white woman, riding in a car built for war service, preaching brotherhood. And last, but not least, these big Black Power people, looking strong
and dangerous as religious fanatics, making black thunder and preaching
black power" (130). When these lines of marchers collide in a chaotic tableau, Ed and Digger are engulfed in the ensuing violence. Himes lingers over
the strange fighting, plucking his detectives from it as looting breaks out in
125th Street.

As *Blind Man with a Pistol* increasingly assumes the form of a political odyssey across the landscape of the 1960s, Himes permits his two detectives a
measure of revelation. Apocalyptic history is revealed to them when they
question the Black Muslim leader, Michael X, who tells them prophetically
that the cause of the Harlem rioting is "Mister Big." Armed with the cryptic
knowledge—that racism has turned even their lives grotesque—Ed and Digger lose all capacity to restore order, much less justice. The blind man who
"didn't want anyone to know he was blind" (222) materializing near the end
of the novel to create pandemonium on a subway train is no more grotesque
than the detectives in the last chapter of the novel.

In chapter 22, which with formal elegance returns to the metaphysical ar-
chitecture Himes created in the first chapter, buildings are being razed on the
north side of 125th Street between Lenox and Seventh avenues to make way
for an urban renewal project. In this half-savage terrain of poisonous air and

crumbling walls, Coffin Ed and Grave Digger idly shoot oversized rats trying to escape into the street. The blind man erupting from the subway exit kills a white cop and in turn is gunned down by three white associates. Again there is rioting, catastrophe without end.

This last of Himes's novels is a sardonic chronicle of the moral corruption and cultural evil that linger over Harlem. The catalog of disasters in *Blind Man with a Pistol,* the razing of a symbolic part of Harlem at the end of the novel and the civil chaos throughout, is a testament to Himes's talent for grotesque art. If much of the comic viciousness of the earlier detective novels has been replaced by stranger and more subtly sinister forms of evil, this is only because the author's maturing vision wanted to focus satirically on the totality of a malignant American power system. Himes had moved from the ethos forced on him by his French publishers who "wanted me to write a Harlem story—'put plenty of comedy into it . . . just an action packed funny story about Harlem.'"[21] From the sweet, steaming exotic Harlem of *For Love of Imabelle,* Himes moved progressively through a dialectical balance of good and evil in the early detective fiction into arresting apocalyptic terrain that permitted him to explore and understand his—and Harlem's—special relationship to American history.

Chapter Seven
Apocalyptic Endings: "Plan B"

By the late 1960s Chester Himes had become obsessed with the constant violence reigning in his archetypal Harlem. For him, this chaos was the emblem of a racist civilization gone stark mad and dragging even Coffin Ed and Grave Digger to deracination. The myriad quasi-political movements that Himes parodies in *Blind Man with a Pistol* fail to achieve liberation for African-Americans because these causes are mercenary, self-serving, integrationist, or debased. That the action of Himes's last complete Harlem thriller takes place on an imaginary Nat Turner Day suggests a radical solution that had been implicit in Himes's fiction for some time: the final holiday for African-Americans can occur only in whirlwind of violent, organized revolution.

In his 1972 interview with Himes in Spain, Hoyt Fuller asked the author if he was writing any new fiction. Himes gave him an extended reply about his plans for "the definitive book on the Black Revolution" (see Appendix). Himes said this would be "a graphic book of what a revolution consists of because . . . this revolution should employ a massive, extreme violence."[1] Coffin Ed, Grave Digger, and the Black Muslim minister Michael X had been moving toward a similar perception of the need for violent revolution to confront the workings of the racist system in *Blind Man with a Pistol*. If Himes's two detectives shoot rats at the end of the novel, it is a psychic response to a profounder knowledge that they should actually be shooting those who have made them victims—the omnipotent white establishment.

Himes's revolutionary novel, tentatively entitled "Plan B," would move one necessary ideological step beyond *Blind Man with a Pistol*. As early as 1969, Himes had confessed in a letter to John Williams, "I have now commenced on the wildest and most defiant of my Harlem series which will wind it up and kill of [*sic*] my two detectives."[2] That same year he acknowledged prophetically, "I have . . . been working on the most violent story I have ever attempted, about an *organized* black rebellion which is extremely bloody and violent, as any such rebellion must be, but unfortunately came unstuck. Anyway, I'm not now finished with it—and then on the other hand it might never be published."[3] The manuscript evolved fitfully; in its rough state "Plan B" is inchoate structurally and stylistically. The moments of brilliance, however, suggest that with revision, "Plan B: A Novel of the Future" would have transcended the Harlem detective cycle by offering a protean revolutionary assessment of America's dark destiny.

Black Protest

In his foreword to *Black on Black* (1973), a collection of earlier short fiction and essays, *Baby Sister*, and two more contemporary short stories, Chester Himes describes himself as a "chauvinistic" writer chiefly obsessed with "Black Protest" and "Black Heterosexuality" (7). In fact, much of the earlier short fiction dealing with black heterosexuality—"A Nigger" (1937), "The Night's for Cryin'" (1937), and "Cotton Gonna Kill Me Yet" (1944) are typical—is undistinguished. Far more original and provocative are the two stories that Himes wrote at end of a prolific career, "Tang" (1967) and "Prediction" (1969). Both were written in Alicante, Spain, at a time when Himes's "thoughts had concentrated on a Black Revolution" and when the author, as he admits in his foreword, "had become firmly convinced that the .only chance Black Americans had of attaining justice and equality in the United States of America was by violence" (7–8). Both, in fact, became parts of the evolving manuscript of "Plan B," although they can stand on their own, especially "Prediction," as distinguished stories.

"Tang," which Himes would position as the first section of the initial chapter in "Plan B," is a ghoulish domestic tragicomedy in which a junkie, T-Bone Smith, kills his wife—the Tang of the title—after a curious altercation. It is summertime in Harlem, and T-Bone in this well-known urban hothouse is described as the grotesque human residue of colonialism and capitalism:

T-Bone was clad only in a pair of greasy pants and his bare black torso was ropy with lean hard muscles and decorated with a variety of scars. His long narrow face was hinged on a mouth with lips the size of automobile tires and the corners of his sloe-shaped eyes were sticky with matter. The short hard burrs on his watermelon head were the color of half-burnt ashes. He had his bare black feet propped up on the kitchen table with the white soles toward the television screen. He was white-mouthed from hunger but was laughing like an idiot at two blackfaced white minstrels on the television screen who earned more money every week by blackening their faces and acting foolish than T-Bone had earned in all his life. (33)

Hungry, destitute, and depraved, T-Bone laughs at a television show that parodies his own slavishness. The affluent white actors with their comic antics perversely expropriate the black experience and profit from it.

T-Bone's woman, Tang, forced by her man into prostitution, is "corroded by vice and hunger," but her eyes remain "red, mean, disillusioned and defiant" (134). Unlike T-Bone, she is not totally submerged by the reality of her oppression but rather retains a nagging consciousness of it—a restless, smoldering awareness of racism and a residual resentment of her husband's own subservience to the white race and exploitation of her. The unexpected arrival of a long, heavy package resembling a box of flowers triggers a personal and ideological conflict between T-Bone and Tang.

This box contains a mysterious rifle resembling an M-14 and a typed note that Tang must read to T-Bone, for he is illiterate: "WARNING!! DO NOT INFORM POLICE!!! Learn your weapon and wait for instructions!!! FREEDOM IS NEAR!!!" (136). The very sight of the M-14 terrifies T-Bone, but Tang is exultant. "It's the uprising, nigger!" she cried. "We gonna be free!" (136). T-Bone, however, contends that he is free and that ownership of the gun jeopardizes that freedom. He insists that they turn the gun over to the police. By contrast, Tang's perception of the power inherent in the rifle is transformational. Never content with selling herself to white men, she suddenly discovers authenticity from behind a rifle barrel; symbolically she is the revolutionary woman prepared to free herself from both racist and sexist fetters.

The character of Tang is somewhat unusual in the vast gallery of women who populate Himes's fiction, for in Tang he theoretically abjures sexist strictures. In creating her as a symbol of the literate revolutionary black woman, Himes conveys a surprising revulsion for the depredations that men— typified by T-Bone and her customers—make against her humanity. Himes's experiment in women's liberation is transitory, however, for although he powerfully conveys the symptoms of a diseased sexism, he reverts to a cynically ironic stance. When T-Bone attempts to grab the rifle from her, Tang pulls the trigger, only to discover that there are no bullets in it. Stoically she meets her destiny, declaring, "I shoulda known, you are whitey's slave; you'll never be free" (138). Unreceptive to the concept of freedom, T-Bone slashes Tang to death.

There is a new critical power and perspective in Himes's fable of revolutionary and antirevolutionary character. His story is a morbid and macabre presentation of the tensions and contradictions inherent in the formation of revolutionary movements. Yet against the conventions of servitude illuminated in Tang, he does set one literate woman who reads a different destiny, if only she can self-ordain it. Himes, however, would have us construe that even greater transformations are needed before an organized rebellion can succeed. Positioning "Tang" at the beginning of his manuscript for "Plan B," he set out to dismantle the doctrine of supremacy that he saw implicit in the American grain.

Predictable Explosions

As a caveat, it must be acknowledged that "Plan B" is a raw, outlandish, uncompleted narrative—a flawed blueprint for the finished revolutionary novel that Himes was never able to finish and revise. It is composed of parts in serious disproportion. Part futuristic prophecy, part conclusion to his Harlem detective cycle, part political and historical fable, part scatological satire in the mode of *Pinktoes*, "Plan B" is a grandiose effort to trace the cultural conditions upon which a black revolution in America can be predicated. Himes's effort to elucidate this revolutionary dialectic is not convincing, in large part because of the crude, blatant, and often conflicting narrative energies that he was unable to harness. In fact, the narrative mixture so misses the mark that we are led to believe that Himes might have had two novels in mind rather than one.[4] It does seem clear that Himes, writing at the end of a turbulent decade, was attempting to find a fundamental strategy for shocking readers into awareness of an appalling national destiny that seemed poised to erupt.

In his interview with Hoyt Fuller, Himes acknowledged that he had been preoccupied with the possibility of a black American revolution ever since his first novel had been published.[5] In fact, the unpredictable explosions governing the psychic and social life of Bob Jones prefigure the more fully developed revolutionary consciousness seen in Himes's second major protagonist, Lee Gordon of *Lonely Crusade*. Himes's second novel was excoriated by leftist critics because of the author's prescient critique of the way in which the American Communist party attempted to manipulate African-American revolutionary fervor for narrow ideological ends. Yet even as he criticized American Communists, Himes remained intrigued by the prospect of violent leftist revolution.

The extreme militancy of Chester Himes appears in its purest form in an essay, "Negro Martyrs Are Needed," that he published in the May 1944 issue of the *Crisis*. This extraordinarily intense article, one of several political essays that Himes wrote during World War II, presages in its revolutionary doctrine the essential themes that the author would attempt to develop in his last effort at fiction, some twenty-five years later. Couched in the rhetoric of America's own democratic revolution, extolling the need for black rebellion in order to guarantee rights under the Constitution, "Negro Martyrs Are Needed" is a quasi-Marxist diatribe against a nation that has made African-Americans "the most oppressed minority group in the world" (*Black on Black*, 231). Himes offers succinct dialectics for the liquidation of colonialist oppression. "(1) Progress can be brought about only by revolution; (2) Revolutions can only be started by incidents; (3) Incidents can be created only by martyrs" (231). Although hoping for white participation in the struggle for democratic equality, Himes considers more probable and valid a "Negro American revolution" that will bring about "the overthrow of our present form of government and the creation of a communistic state" (231).

When Grave Digger and Coffin Ed are first on the scene to cover the murder of Tang in "Plan B," there is evidence of this vocabulary of violent revolution in the mysterious gun—altered so that the authorities will never be able to trace it—and note. Yet Digger and Coffin Ed do not sense revolutionary sublimity in the scene—just a horribly mutilated dead woman. In blind fury, Grave Digger bludgeons T-Bone to death with the butt of his long nickel-plated pistol. This scarcely revolutionary act of violence results in Digger's suspension. Shortly thereafter, Coffin Ed takes a leave from the force in order to recuperate from a badly bruised kneecap. Himes, apparently starting another detective story in his cycle, abandons his heroes for a larger problem in detection: why was the automatic rifle sent to an ignorant black man? From the chaotic and absurd disorder of what the authorities prefer to treat as a local "nigger mess," Himes shifts his novel radically to the landscape of violent revolution.

Himes juxtaposes the random, self-destructive violence of the action in chapter 1 of "Plan B," against the more purposeful revolutionary violence that unfolds in the grotesque domain of the second chapter. Himes's view of his developing novel does not depend on any of his previous models but on an evolving dynamic of disparate parts that seem to exhaust themselves. Thus chapter 2, comprised of five parts, offers a prolegomenon for race warfare. Coffin Ed and Grave Digger have disappeared from the novel, but the landscape remains the same as in the detective novels. It is 11:30 P.M. on Eighth Avenue in Harlem, and it is hot. It is ten days after the murder of Tang and Digger's summary execution of T-Bone.

We immediately recognize the contingent absurdity of Himes's slum setting, but in "Plan B" his tendency to editorialize, almost like a revolutionary pamphleteer, is acute. The heightened urban vertigo—the heated and deracinated sense of the ghetto population as woefully corrupt—is far more squalid to Himes "than the squalor of the black ghettos in Rio de Janeiro, Miami, Capetown [sic], even Watts."[6] We now have systemic urban decline within a comparative global framework, with Himes, in a hieratic mode, overindulging the reader's senses in the stench of the scene: "It stank from the years' accumulations of thousands of unlisted odors embedded in the crumbling walls, the rotting linoleum, the decayed wall paper, the sweaty garments, the incredible perfumes, the rancid face creams and cooking fats, the toe jams, the bad breath from rotting or dirty teeth, the pistules of pus" (29). This sentence, embedded in a far more extensive paragraph that offers an inventory of Harlem filth and stench, is exaggerated in order to push Himes's thesis into the realm of grotesque probability. In such an irrationally, metaphysically loathsome world, an explosive revolution should be predictable.

Because the urban squalor is so dehumanizing and irrational, the radical solution seems to be violent revolution. Out of the night, a man shooting from a tenement window kills two white policemen patrolling the streets—an act precipitating a massive police invasion of primitive intensity. The whole second chapter is a grotesque reverie on the stimulus of violence as the "half-naked brother" shoots at the police "as though they were scavenger birds" (32), while the black citizens in "panicstricken terror" cower in doorways and hallways. Ultimately a police tank "shaped like a turtle with an insect's antenna" (37) systematically demolishes the tenement and the black revolutionary. In the melee, fifty-nine black citizens and five white police are killed. Even in the aftermath of official investigations and white remorse, Himes erects another macabre episode in which a black spectator attending an outdoor concert of *Porgy and Bess* is lynched grotesquely by a motorcycle gang. The constituents of a black revolution have now been outlined by Himes—not so much portentously as with debonair and comic buoyancy.

Race Warfare

"Plan B" is about the exercise of power by white America and the mysterious revolutionary network that arises to combat it. In the third chapter, spasmodic violence occurs throughout the United States in the wake of the events in New York. Blacks shoot at whites in Mississippi, Washington, D.C., San Francisco, Chicago, Cleveland, and elsewhere. Striving for an absurdist tapestry of destruction, Himes resorts all too frequently to facile humor, offering comic-book frames of mayhem, as when a B-52 bomber is sent to destroy the Cuyahoga County Jail, where a black administrator of the Department of Health, Education and Welfare has been systematically killing all white prisoners and officials. Sharp, grotesque effects now seem largely beyond the reach of Himes's syntax as he strives to convey the totality of the American racial experience in his futuristic novel.

With race warfare and the severest reprisals—tantamount to genocide—sweeping the United States, Himes attempts to investigate the historic sources of American racial conflict but with increasingly uneven results. America, after all, owes its peculiar history to the reality and legacy of slavery. Thus Himes, in a long, meandering fourth chapter, examines the origins and aftermath of slavery through the particular destiny of "Chitterlings, Inc.— the home of the fish-fed pig" (95). This largest of all black enterprises in America, presided over by the charismatic leader Tomsson Black, is located in swampland bordering Mobile Bay, a southern locale Himes establishes so that he can explore his historic theme from one center of corruption.

Obviously Himes wanted "The Birth of Chitterlings" section to serve as a paradigm to hold the fatal ironies and incongruities of slavery that stretch from the American past to its present (Himes makes constant allusions to Vietnam) and into the future. Himes, however, does not make any astute perceptions about America's racial predicament. In fact, this section suffers from a combination of poor southern gothic machinery culled from Faulkner and a soft pornography reminiscent of Erskine Caldwell. Incest, rape, and murder—the trinity of the southern gothic style—predominate as the land passes from white to black ownership in a historical continuum of more than 150 years. It is clear that Himes would like to trace the origins of American racism not so much to economics as to perverse psychosexual drives. It is equally clear from the poorly conceived narrative stretches involving white and black sexuality that he did not have the artistic control to do justice to a potentially great theme.

Tomsson Black, whose own background includes participation in the radical causes of the 1960s and imprisonment on false charges of rape, is the genius of the revolution, the bankroller of the guns sent anonymously to black American males. Now a reformed capitalist, he is so successful as to be trusted implicitly by white America and thus almost beyond suspicion. His accomodationist press conferences reassure a distraught nation, even as he schemes to bring down the Republic.

Only Grave Digger and Coffin Ed suspect Tomsson Black, but they cannot convince the white establishment. Fired now from the New York police force, they stalk Black on their own. Himes never wrote the later three or four chapters of "Plan B" that would have fleshed out these episodes, but a synopsis remains, suggesting at least two endings. In the first, the aging detectives gain a confession from Tomsson Black but argue over arresting him; Digger kills Ed and Black in turn liquidates Digger so that the revolution can continue.[7] Yet on an alternate separate page, Himes has Black, Grave Digger, and Ed kidnap the president and vice president.[8] The armed rebellion has failed, but now they hold America's two chief executives "for a ransom of freedom."

Chester Himes, already declining in health as he wrote "Plan B," probably never would have recovered the resources of language and narrative control that would have enabled him to complete and then revise the novel. The futuristic environment of the novel lacks the deft satire of a Kurt Vonnegut operating in a similar apocalyptic mode in his best fiction, from *Cat's Cradle* to *Slaughterhouse Five*. Nevertheless, there is a visionary and demonic power in the two excerpts that Himes was able to revise and publish in *Black on Black*. Just as "Tang" introduces the novel, a second remarkable story, "Prediction," appearing as a fifth section in chapter 4 of "Plan B," offers the author's most appallingly grotesque vision of a nation from which he could never totally disengage himself.

"Prediction"

"Prediction" represents the final perfection of Himes's grotesque style and the consummation of his radical vision. Detached from the uneven matrix of "Plan B," it is a minor achievement in the history of American short fiction. In significant ways the story confirms the premise of Himes's earlier essay, "Negro Martyrs Are Needed": that violent black revolution can bring down the American capitalist state.

The story is a savagely cold evocation of a future world where the colonialist and capitalist conditions of American society result in chaos. It begins with a police parade up Main Street of a big city. That Himes focuses on the archetypal main street of a nameless metropolis suggests that he is preoccupied with a national topology that can catch the contradictions of American culture. The white race is on parade, for none of the 5,000 marching policemen is black. The crowd, too, is entirely white, denying "that a black race existed" (*Black on Black*, 280). The only black presence is an armed janitor, hidden in an unlighted chamber of the city's Catholic cathedral, staring down a narrow slot in the stone walls and patiently awaiting the parade.

Himes creates in his unarmed revolutionary figure a sort of dark God who undercuts, by his very presence in a Christian church, the colonialist Christ. Himes writes that "he had waited four hundred years for this moment and he was not in a hurry" (252). The shrouded figure is the lethal embodiment of what D. H. Lawrence declared was the essence of the American soul: hard, stoical, murderous. Yet Lawrence was speaking of Natty Bumppo, while Himes erects a parody of the white trailblazer—a black revolutionary prophet who will lay waste to an urban American wilderness. Looking at this situation from a slightly different perspective, Bruce Franklin, who aptly terms the story a parable, declares that "Himes is finally able to exorcise the image of the Catholic church—by converting it into a sanctuary of armed Black rebellion."[9]

The humble revolutionary, who refuses to make the sign of the cross in a white Christian church, is Himes's Negro martyr, an individual who knows the inevitability of his own death but is "consoled by the hope" that his violent assertion "would make life safer for the blacks in the future" (282). Straddling the church's poor box—a deft emblem of his power to crush the Christian capitalist culture—the janitor wills his intelligence, his soul, toward a particular direction of force. This direction is toward liberation: "To take the decisions, to think for himself, to die without application" (253). Revolutionary thought opens this individual to the power of the self.

Himes's nameless black man coldly personifies the revolutionary will. As the long, symmetrical lines of the police parade march into his sight, he begins to demolish them with bursts from his automatic rifle. From the lightly ironic, lightly introspective tonalities of the opening paragraphs, Himes moves to the grotesque landscape he had mined so successfully in his earlier fiction as his new revolutionary man wreaks appallingly absurd havoc on the epitome of the American political state.

The first burst, passing from left to right, made a row of entries in the faces of the five officers in the lead. The first officers were of the same height and holes appeared in their upper cheekbones just beneath the eyes and in the bridges of their noses. Snot mixed with blood exploded from their nostrils and their caps flew off behind, suddenly filled with fragments of their skulls and pasty gray brain matter streaked with capillaries like gobs of putty finely laced with red ink. The commissioner, who was slightly shorter, was hit in both temples and both eyes, and the bullets made star-shaped entries in both the lenses of his spectacles and the corneas of his eyeballs and a gelatinous substance heavily mixed with blood spurted from the rims of his eye sockets. He wore no hat to catch his brains and fragments of skull, and they exploded through the sunny atmosphere and splattered the spectators with goo, tufts of gray hair and splinters of bone. One skull fragment, larger than the others struck a tall, well-dressed man on the cheek, cutting the skin and splashing brains against his face like a custard pie in a Mack Sennett comedy. The two chiefs on the far side, being a shade taller than the others, caught the bullets in their teeth. These latter suffered worse, if such a thing was possible. Bloodstained teeth flew through the air like exotic insects, a shattered denture was expelled forward from a shattered jaw like the puking of plastic food. Jawbones came unhinged and dangled from shattered mouths. But the ultimate damage was that the heads were cut off just above the bottom jaws, which swung grotesquely from headless bodies spouting blood like gory fountains. (283–84)

The police massacre is heightened to demonic proportions, with Himes relying once again on principles of grotesque artistry to reveal objectively the terrifying and alien features of American culture.

The hecatomb that Himes imagines in "Prediction" is bizarre in its dimensions. He litters the streets with grisly, squashy shards of humanity, reducing white culture to "bits of exploded viscera, stuffed intestines bursting with half-chewed ham and cabbage and rice and gravy . . . lying in the gutters like pork sausages before knotting" (285). Himes's reductionist techniques of the grotesque, his ability to transform human beings into lesser parts and objects, is his absurd way of dissecting the pathologies—even the diets—of bourgeois society. For the black assassin, the sight of these brains flying upward to heaven induces "spiritual ecstasy," for he senses that he is freeing himself finally from historical contingencies.

The black assailant has entered another world of existence through his carefully planned violence. He has literally and symbolically stepped out of ordinary, racist existence, triggering a "few minutes of macabre comedy" in which hundreds of whites—police and spectators—are killed either by him or by the wild self-destructive police counterfire. Ultimately a police tank has to destroy a central bulwark of its own culture—the church itself—before the black assassin is silenced. Nevertheless one black revolutionary has shattered the placid domain of American public life:

In the wake of this bloody massacre the stock market crashed. The dollar fell on the whole market. The very structure of capitalism began to crumble. Confidence in the capitalistic system had an almost fatal shock. All over the world millions of capitalists sought means to invest their wealth in the East.

Good night. (287)

Himes's nationalist fantasy ends with this short two-word coda, almost as if he laconically believes that his "prediction" is indeed the direction the world might take.

Chester Himes wanted "Plan B" to serve as his final and most revolutionary public document. Yet in *My Life of Absurdity* he admits that by 1970 the manuscript "was gradually heading for disaster" (363). Indeed Himes could not sustain his grotesque vision of a second American revolution or even figure out its metaphysics coherently. Within the more controlled latitudes of "Tang" and "Prediction," he does manage to create antithetical versions of the revolutionary and counterrevolutionary self. Moreover, the grotesque discontinuities in American culture that he exposes emblematically in "Prediction" constitute one of his finest, most ferocious, and most lucid narratives. Unable

to find a proper form or voice for his larger nationalistic fantasy, "Plan B,"
Chester Himes abandoned the effort—and all fiction writing—to concen-
trate in the 1970s on the completion of his autobiography.[10]

Chapter Eight
Final Assessment

Before his death in 1984, Chester Himes had to pay many times for his personal and public, literary and ideological sins. Praise for his early work was grudging, as when James Baldwin in an otherwise negative review of *Lonely Crusade* acknowledged the novel's "flashes of power and insight."[1] Later in his career, Himes was accused of abandoning serious fiction for crime potboilers. Ironically these "potboilers" placed Himes in temporary vogue, first in France and then in the United States, but he never earned enough money from his publishers or Hollywood to be spoiled by fame. Indeed his vigorous, cynical, hard-boiled contempt for America's culture of violence, his exile, and his irascible relationships with his contemporaries seemingly predestined an obscure ending.

Himes's sins may be buried with him, but this is not so of his reputation. Fortunately he always had persevering admirers. For example, in 1962, Carl Van Vechten observed that Himes "introduced the homosexual theme long before Baldwin was ever heard of."[2] John Williams, although Himes would have a few unkind words to say about him in *My Life of Absurdity*, generously termed the renegade expatriate America's greatest living naturalistic writer. If nothing more, the genius of Chester Himes changed the landscape of American detective fiction. Yet there is more. For almost forty years, Himes wrote about the violent absurdities of American and international culture from unique perspectives. His radical reading of the nation and his persistently absurdist vision make him a special purveyor of the American experience.

Himes once declared that he had been born of bourgeois parents, and "that finishes that."[3] It was Himes's peculiar destiny to be renounced by bourgeois culture for multitudinous sins and, in turn, to condemn and renounce the theory of American life posited by bourgeois society. Himes had a marked inability to contend with a social structure that was deplorably racist in its bourgeois achievements. His vocation as a writer was an enabling effort to deal with and transcend his place in this world. Moreover, Himes deliberately conceived and developed an imaginative art and theory of the grotesque in fiction to expose and subdue the anarchic impulses spawned by American culture.

From his first novel, *If He Hollers Let Him Go*, to his unfinished "Plan B," Himes maintains that the deepest desire of American culture is to be rid of the African-American. The paradox of white America's having "aliens" in its midst who cannot be permitted to assimilate and yet who will not go away explains the demonic energy that animates Himes's fiction and drives his obsessive characters. Himes never relaxed his strenuous objection to this banal, bourgeois sense of American privilege, nor did he ever reconcile himself to his own family's foundering on the jagged edge of the American dream. In fact, the more truly bizarre his condemnation of the quirks in American life, the more accomplished is Himes's work.

Sadly, Himes's talent was often too rushed by circumstances for its own good. At its worst, as in the melodramatic endings of *Lonely Crusade* and *The Third Generation*, there is only a marginal sense of formal and stylistic control. Yet when Himes seizes the diverse possibilities of the grotesque style, controlling bizarre juxtapositions of images and incidents, he produces striking effects corresponding to the radical energy of his vision. His finest achievement in this mode of writing is his cycle of detective fiction. In fact, Himes is the aesthetic counterpart of his two detectives, stalking the dark streets of America like a cat. In *Blind Man with a Pistol*, there is a paradigmatic scene in which Grave Digger and Coffin Ed "were idling along, west on 123rd Street, with the lights out as was their custom on dark side streets. The car scarcely made a sound; for all its dilapidated appearance the motor was ticking almost silently. It passed along practically unseen, like a ghostly vehicle floating in the dark, its occupants invisible" (43). Within the serpentine cadences of this passage, there is the interweaving image of the invisible author, never content with his anonymity within American society, always the master of grotesque art, prepared to spring bizarre, apocalyptic tricks on a recalcitrant public.

By means of grotesque art, Himes aligns himself with a tradition of absurdist fiction that has both European and American antecedents. When Constance Rourke in 1931 identified the essence of much American humor as a "median between terror and laughter which is grotesque," she properly acknowledged an animating impulse not only in southwestern tales but in a tradition that we can trace through Poe, Melville, Twain, Faulkner, West, Ellison, and O'Connor to the contemporary period.[4] Himes in his later European phase produced fiction as exaggerated in its comic terror and violence as anything in Faulkner—an author who was, Himes wrote in his autobiography, a constant source of bizarre inspiration. Moreover, Himes connects generically with the European tradition of the grotesque. His broad references to Sartre and Camus and such pointed declarations that Richard

Wright's later fiction would have been more successful had it been more absurd point to his aesthetic allegiances. The Rabelaisian scenes in *The Primitive* and *Pinktoes*, the Kafkaesque absurdities of the trial in *A Case of Rape*, the Dostoyevskian labyrinth that is Harlem in the detective cycle—all point to Himes's place with the world of extremities framed by the tradition of the grotesque.

Ultimately Chester Himes takes us into the bizarre labyrinth of American culture, undercutting it with satiric savagery and parody. Bob Jones's grotesque dreams in *If He Hollers Let Him Go* are the embryonic emblem of the larger nightmare of racial genocide that Himes attempted to orchestrate in "Plan B." Between his first and last novels, Himes invited readers to pursue him through other archetypal labyrinths—the prison, the ghetto, the segregated world. That Himes could locate uproariously comic scenes within a profoundly flawed and tragic world explains his rare literary imagination. What Himes imagines is also what the author lived and endured, and this takes us back to him.

Chester Himes never got over the impact of racism on his life, never accommodated himself to it, and this explains his own hateful passions and destructive gusto. In 1970 he wrote to John Williams, "I'm still having trouble with this Spanish kind of racism. . . . Anyway there's nothing much else I can do now—too old and tired. . . . I'll just sit here and try to write the rest of my autobiography."[5] At Casa Griot (the name of a beloved cat and a term used to describe the storyteller in an African village) in Moraira, Himes worked out his own form of immortality. In the last line of his autobiography, he resigns himself to a life and a world that have not been lost: "For all its inconsistencies, its contradictions, its humiliations, its triumphs, its failures, its tragedies, its hurts, its ecstasies and its absurdities; that's my life—the third generation out of slavery." It will be left to a new generation of critics—as Ishmael Reed has suggested—to assess the legacy of Chester B. Himes.

Appendix
Himes on the Black Revolution*

I began writing this book when I first came to Paris. I started to write the definitive book on the Black Revolution, a graphic book of what a revolution consists of because I have the actual details, scenes, and the actual story of what's been done. I have always believed—and this was from the time that *If He Hollers* . . . was published—that the Black man in America should mount a serious revolution and this revolution should employ a massive, extreme violence. This is based on the assumption Black people want to do it. I believe that this would change the conditions of the Black man in America, if he would mount a violent revolution in the West; that would be of benefit to two-three million people. If the Black man would mount a revolution that would result in the death of three million people—even if most, or at least two-thirds, were Black people themselves, it would still change the position of the Black man in America or in the world. Because I believe the Black man in America holds the destiny of the entire Western world. He holds the destiny in his hands because a study of the economy of the world will show you that if America fails as a nation then all the white Western world will fail, and the Eastern world will move in and take over. If this ever happens, which I don't think is possible, but if they did mount a revolution in force, then all the institutions would collapse. The economy of America would be the first to collapse. The American dollar even in the series of riots which happened a couple years ago—the dollar slid on the world market; the people lost confidence in the whole American economy, and all the nations in the world were getting ready to jump away from America and let it sink. America is the nation that keeps the Western world alive economically. So once the institutions and the economic system in America fails, the Blacks are going to fail. But if they use this extraordinary power, they must not be deterred by the white community sheltering them. Because the white community has worked out a very thorough system in which they will play with the Black community. . . . This is a game played with intricate skill if the Blacks would reject that game together—reject the whole idea—just say they're tired of the game, we don't

---

*From Hoyt W. Fuller, "Traveller on a Long, Rough, Lonely Old Road: An Interview with Chester Himes," *Black World* 21 (March 1972): 18.

want you doing it, and then move in force against the entire white structure, then America, to save its economic structure, its capitalistic structure, will give anybody anything. They'll give the Black man his equality and everything else to save the American way of life and economic structure in the world. They'll make these concessions and do anything. They're doing it now. They're trying to find out how they can do it without suffering any damage to their economic system. They're ready right now to ship the South Vietnamese out and gobble anybody else. There's no ideology involved in the American movements in the world. They're just trying to protect themselves and trying to protect their way of life, and if it is challenged, the only people who can challenge it thoroughly are the Blacks themselves.

Notes and References

Chapter One

1. Chester Himes, *Blind Man with a Pistol* (New York: William Morrow, 1969), n.p.
2. Michael Millgate, *American Social Fiction: James to Cozzens* (New York: Barnes and Noble, 1964), 196.
3. In *The Grotesque in Art and Literature* (Bloomington: Indiana University Press, 1963), Wolfgang Kayser traces the demonic and alienative elements as twin constituents of the grotesque.
4. Chester Himes, *The Quality of Hurt: The Autobiography of Chester Himes*, vol. 1 (Garden City, N.Y.: Doubleday, 1972), 4. Subsequent references, cited parenthetically in the text, are to this edition.
5. Himes to John A. Williams, 31 October 1962, John A. Williams Collection, University of Rochester Library.
6. Roger Rosenblatt, "Black Autobiography: Life as a Death Weapon," *Yale Review* 65 (1976):521. For more extended treatments, see Stephen Butterfield, *Black Autobiography in America* (Amherst: University of Massachusetts Press, 1974); Sidonie Smith, *Where I'm Bound: Patterns of Slavery and Freedom in Black American Autobiography* (Westport, Conn.: Greenwood Press, 1974); and Robert B. Stepto, *From Behind the Veil: A Study of Afro-American Narrative* (Urbana: University of Illinois Press, 1979).
7. For a useful evaluation of Himes's early fiction, see Stephen F. Milliken, *Chester Himes: A Critical Appraisal* (Columbia: University of Missouri Press, 1976), 31–69.
8. St. Clair Drake, Introduction to Claude McKay, *A Long Way from Home: An Autobiography* (New York: Harcourt, Brace and World, 1970), x.
9. See B. A. Botkin, *Lay My Burden Down: A Folk History of Slavery* (Chicago: University of Chicago Press, 1945), 60.
10. Ralph Ellison, *Shadow and Act* (New York: Random House, 1964), 78. For a brilliant elucidation of the blues motif, see Elizabeth Schultz, "To Be Black and Blue: The Blues Genre in Black American Autobiography," *Kansas Quarterly* 7 (Summer 1975):81–96.
11. Himes, *My Life of Absurdity: The Autobiography of Chester Himes*, vol. 2 (Garden City, N.Y.: Doubleday, 1976), 1. Subsequent references, cited parenthetically in the text, are to this edition.
12. James Lundquist, *Chester Himes* (New York: Frederick Ungar, 1976), 93.
13. John A. Williams, "Chester Himes—My Man Himes," in *Flashbacks: A Twenty-Year Diary of Article Writing* (Garden City, N.Y.: Doubleday, 1974), 298.

14. Roger Rosenblatt, "Black Autobiography," in James Olney, ed., *Autobiography: Essays Theoretical and Critical* (Princeton, N.J.: Princeton University Press, 1980), 172.

15. Quoted by Himes in *My Life of Absurdity*, 195–96.

16. *Publisher's Weekly*, 30 November 1984, 29.

Chapter Two

1. Williams, "Chester Himes," 19.

2. Himes to John A. Williams, 31 October 1962, Williams Collection. In this letter Himes writes of *If He Hollers Let Him Go*: "It was my original intention to write a mystery story wherein white people were getting killed all over town and no one could conceive of the motive. The motive was simply the compulsion making a Negro kill white people because they were white. . . . But it turned out differently and became *If He Hollers*."

3. Chester B. Himes, *If He Hollers Let Him Go* (Garden City, N.Y.: Doubleday, Doran & Co., 1945), 9. Subsequent references, cited parenthetically in the text, are to this edition.

4. Noel Schraufnagel, *From Apology to Protest: The Black American Novel* (Deland, Fla.: Everett/Edwards, 1973), 37.

5. Edward Margolies, *Native Sons: A Critical Study of Twentieth Century Negro Authors* (Philadelphia: J. B. Lippincott Co., 1968), 90.

6. See Chester Himes, "Zoot Suit Riots Are Race Riots," *Crisis* 50 (July 1943):20.

7. Addison Gayle, Jr., in *The Way of the New World: The Black Novel in America* (Garden City, N. Y.: Doubleday, 1975), observes that *If He Hollers Let Him Go* is "concerned with the powerlessness of the black middle-class intellectual" (182).

8. Roger Rosenblatt, *Black Fiction* (Cambridge: Harvard University Press, 1974), 167.

9. Himes to John A. Williams, 31 October 1962, Williams Collection.

10. For a representative sampling of Himes's polemical essays of the 1940s, see his *Black on Black* (New York: Doubleday, 1973), 213–35. Subsequent references, cited parenthetically in the text, are to this edition.

11. Chester Himes, *Lonely Crusade* (New York: Alfred A. Knopf, 1947), 15. Subsequent references, cited parenthetically in the text, are to this edition.

12. See, for example, Milliken, *Chester Himes*, 98.

Chapter Three

1. Chester Himes, "The Dilemma of the Negro Artist in the United States," in John A. Williams, ed., *Beyond the Angry Black* (New York: Cooper Square Publishing, 1969), 52.

2. See "Crazy in the Stir," *Esquire* 2 (August 1934):23, 114–16; "To What

Red Hell," *Esquire* 2 (October 1934):100–01, 122, 127;"The Visiting Hour," *Esquire* 7 (January 1937):64, 146–48; "Every Opportunity," *Esquire* 7 (May 1937): 99, 129–30. Himes also published several prison stories in *Abbott's Monthly and Illustrated News* (Chicago): "His Last Day," (November 1932):33, 61–63; "Prison Mass," (March 1933):36, 37, 61–64; (April 1933):20, 21, 48–46; (May 1933): 37, 61, 62; and "I Don't Want to Die," (October 1933):20–21.

    3. Himes to Richard Wright, 19 October 1952, Beinecke Library.

    4. Himes to Carl Van Vechten, 18 February 1947, Beinecke Library.

    5. Chester Himes, *Cast the First Stone* (Chatham, N.J.: Chatham Bookseller, 1973), 17. Subsequent references, cited parenthetically in the text, are to this edition.

    6. H. Bruce Franklin, "Two Novelists of the American Prison," in *The Victim as Criminal and Artist: Literature from the American Prison* (New York: Oxford University Press, 1978), 212.

    7. Walter, J. Ong, "On Saying We and Us to Literature," in Houston A. Baker, Jr., ed., *Three American Literatures* (New York: Modern Language Association of America, 1982), 3.

    8. Milliken, *Chester Himes: A Critical Appraisal*, 160.

    9. Lundquist, *Chester Himes*, 73–74.

    10. Franklin, "Two Novelists," 222.

    11. See, for instance, W. R. Burnett's review in *Saturday Review of Literature*, 17 January 1953, where he confesses, "I'll admit I'm prejudiced and that prejudice makes for false assumptions"(14).

    12. "*Yesterday Will Make You Cry*," Manuscript Collection, Beinecke Library, p. 456.

    13. Sealed letters from Rico to Himes are deposited in the Beinecke Library.

    14. For an incisive analysis of this story, see Franklin, "Two Novelists," 215ff.

Chapter Four

    1. John Williams, "Chester Himes—My Man Himes," 336.

    2. See, for example, Riley Hughes, review of *The Third Generation* by Chester Himes, *Catholic World* (April 1954):72. Hughes writes,"Through tying his story to a Freudian mother complex formula, ruthlessly applied, Mr. Himes removes his characters as far from the reader's sympathy as they are from convincing reality."

    3. Himes to Carl Van Vechten, 23 November 1952, Beinecke Library.

    4. Chester Himes, *The Third Generation* (Chatham, N.J.: Chatham Bookseller, 1973), 349. Subsequent page references, cited parenthetically in the text, are to this edition.

    5. Ellison, *Shadow and Act*, 148.

    6. For perceptive and largely revisionist evaluations of this literature, see Herbert G. Gutman, "Persistent Myths about the Afro-American Family," in Michael Gordon, ed., *The American Family in Social-Historical Perspective*, 3d ed. (New York: St. Martin's Press, 1983), 459–81; Jualynne Dodson, "Conceptualiza-

tions of Black Families," in Harriette McAdoo, *Black Families* (Newberry Park, Calif.: Sage, 1988), 23–35.

7. Dodson, "Conceptualizations," 27.

8. Robert B. Stepto, *From Behind the Veil: A Study of Afro American Narrative* (Urbana: University of Illinois Press, 1979), ix.

9. Frank Kermode, *The Sense of an Ending: Studies in the Theory of Fiction* (London: Oxford University Press, 1966), 133.

Chapter Five

1. Williams, "Chester Himes," 313.

2. Himes, "Reading Your Own," *New York Times Book Review*, 4 June 1967, 7, hereafter cited parenthetically in the text.

3. Hoyt W. Fuller, "Traveler on the Long, Rough, Lonely Old Road: An Interview with Chester Himes," *Black World* (March 1972):20.

4. Chester Himes, *La Fin d'un primitif* (Paris: Gallimard, 1956), 8, my translation, hereafter cited parenthetically in the text.

5. Edward Margolies, *Native Sons: A Critical Study of Twentieth Century Black American Authors* (Philadelphia: J. B. Lippincott, 1968), 93.

6. Milliken, *Chester Himes: A Critical Appraisal*, 185.

7. Himes, *The Primitive* (New York: New American Library, 1955), 24. Subsequent page references, cited parenthetically in the text, are to this edition.

8. Himes to Williams, C. 1963, Williams Collection.

9. Ibid., 11 October 1962, Williams Collection.

10. Ibid., 31 October 1962, 5, 7 Williams Collection.

11. Jervis Anderson, *This Was Harlem, 1900–1950* (New York: Farrar Straus and Giroux, 1982), 343.

12. Chester Himes, *Pinktoes* (New York: G. P. Putnam's, 1965), 24. Subsequent page references, cited parenthetically in the text, are to this edition.

13. Chester Himes, *A Case of Rape* (Washington, D.C.: Howard University Press, 1984), 28. Subsequent page references, cited parenthetically in the text, are to this edition.

14. *Le Harlem de Chester Himes* (Quebec, Canada: Editions Naaman, 1978), 70, my translation.

15. Himes to John A. Williams, 11 October 1962, Williams Collection.

16. Quoted by Michel Fabre in "Dissecting Western Pathology: A Critique—*A Case of Rape*," *Black World* (March 1972):43.

17. Ibid., 48.

Chapter Six

1. See Edward Margolies, "The Thrillers of Chester Himes," *Studies in Black Literature* (June 1970):10.

2. Williams, "Chester Himes—My Man Himes," 315.

3. Himes, *For Love of Imabelle* (Chatham, N.J.: Chatham Bookseller, 1973), 111. Subsequent references, cited parenthetically in the text, are to this edition.

4. Himes, *Run Man Run* (Garden City, N.Y.: Doubleday, 1973), 7. Subsequent references, cited parenthetically in the text, are to this edition.

5. *The Heat's On* (New York: G. P. Putnam's, 1966), 3. Subsequent references, cited parenthetically in the text, are to this edition.

6. Himes, *Cotton Comes to Harlem* (New York: G.P. Putnam's, 1965), 48–49. Subsequent references, cited parenthetically in the text, are to this edition.

7. Kenneth B. Clark, *Dark Ghetto: Dilemmas of Social Power* (New York: Harper & Row, 1965), 11.

8. Williams, "Chester Himes—My Man Himes," 314.

9. Edward Margolies, *Which Way Did He Go?* (New York: Holmes and Meier, 1982), 2.

10. Franklin, *The Victim as Criminal and Artist*, 224.

11. Himes, *The Real Cool Killers* (Chatham, N.J.: Chatham Bookseller, 1973), 15. Subsequent references, cited parenthetically in the text, are to this edition.

12. Margolies, "Thrillers," p. 59.

13. *All Shot Up* (Chatham, N.J.: Chatham Bookseller, 1973), 17. Subsequent references, cited parenthetically in the text, are to this edition.

14. Julian Symons, *Bloody Murder: From the Detective Story to the Crime Novel* (London: Faber and Faber, 1972), 201.

15. Himes, *The Crazy Kill* (Chatham, N.J.: Chatham Bookseller, 1973), 6. Subsequent page references, cited parenthetically in the text, are to this edition.

16. Himes, *The Big Gold Dream* (New York: New American Library, 1975), 9. Subsequent references, cited parenthetically in the text, are to this edition.

17. Dennis Porter, *The Pursuit of Crime: Art and Ideology in Detective Fiction* (New Haven: Yale University Press, 1981), 29.

18. Williams, "Chester Himes—My Man Himes," 306.

19. Fred Pfeil, "Policiers Noirs," *Nation*, 15 November 1986, 524.

20. Lundquist, *Chester Himes*, 117.

21. Himes to Carl Van Vechten, 16 December 1954, Beinecke Library.

Chapter Seven

1. Fuller, "Traveler on the Long, Rough, Lonely Old Road," 18–19.

2. Himes to John Williams, 6 February 1969, Williams Collection.

3. Ibid., 15 April 1969, Williams Collection.

4. One part of the manuscript has the title "The Birth of Chitterlings, Inc." and begins pagination with "p. 1." Himes tried unsuccessfully to fit it into "Plan B" as a fifty-nine-page fourth chapter in a projected nine-chapter work.

5. Fuller, "Traveler on the Long, Rough, Lonely Old Road."

6. Himes, "Plan B: A Novel of the Future," 25. This unpublished manuscript was shared with the author by John A. Williams. Page references are to this copy.

7. Ibid., 26–27.

8. In *My Life of Absurdity*, Himes offers this ending: "I began writing a book called *Plan B*, about a real black revolution in which my two black detectives split up and eventually Grave Digger kills Coffin Ed to save the cause" (361).

9. Franklin, *The Victim as Criminal and Artist*, 230.

10. A French translation of "Plan B" exists, published by Lieu Commun (Paris, 1983).

Chapter Eight

1. James Baldwin, "History as Nightmare," *New Leader* 25 October 1947, 15.

2. Carl Van Vechten to John Williams, October 1962, Williams Collection.

3. Himes to Carl Brandt, 25 October 1962, in Williams Collection.

4. Constance Rourke, *American Humor: A Study of National Character* (New York: Harcourt Brace and Co., 1931), 49.

5. Himes to John A. Williams, 23 June 1970, Williams Collection.

Selected Bibliography

PRIMARY WORKS

Novels

All Shot Up. New York: Avon, 1960; reprint ed., Chatham, N.J.: Chatham Bookseller, 1973. In French, *Imbroglio negro.* Translated by J. Fillion. Paris: Gallimard, 1960. Originally titled "Don't Play with Death."

The Big Gold Dream. New York: Avon, 1960; reprint ed., Chatham, N.J.: Chatham Bookseller, 1973. In French, *Tout pour plait.* Translated by Ives Malartic. Paris: Gallimard, 1959.

Blind Man with a Pistol. New York: William Morrow, 1969. Published as *Hot Day Hot Night.* New York: Dell, 1970. In French, *L'Aveugle au pistolet.* Translated by Henri Robillot. Paris: Gallimard, 1970.

A Case of Rape. Washington, D.C.: Howard University Press, 1984. In French, *Une Affaire de viol.* Translated by André Mathieu. Paris: Editions les yeux ouverts, 1963.

Cast the First Stone. New York: New American Library, 1952. Originally titled "Black Sheep."

Cotton Comes to Harlem. New York: G. P. Putnam's Sons, 1965. In French, *Retour en Afrique.* Translated by Pierre Sergent. Paris: Plon, 1964. (Filmed by Samuel Goldwyn, Jr., and distributed by United Artists in 1970).

The Crazy Kill. New York: Avon Books, 1959; reprint ed., Chatham, N.J.: Chatham Bookseller, 1973. In French, *Couche dans le pain.* Translated by J. Herisson and Henri Robillot. Paris: Gallimard, 1959. Originally titled "A Jealous Man Can't Win."

For Love of Imabelle. New York: Fawcett, 1957. Published as *A Rage in Harlem.* New York: Avon, 1965; reprint ed., Chatham, N.J.: Chatham Bookseller, 1973. In French, *La Reine des pommes.* Translated by Minnie Danzas. Paris: Gallimard, 1958. Titled originally "The Five-Cornered Square."

The Heat's On. New York: G. P. Putnam's, 1966. Published as *Come Back, Charleston Blue.* New York: Dell, 1967. In French, *Ne nous enervons pas.* Translated by J. Fillion. Paris: Gallimard, 1961. (Filmed by Samuel Goldwyn, Jr., with title *Come Back, Charleston Blue*, and distributed by United Artists in 1974.)

If He Hollers Let Him Go. New York: Doubleday, 1945.

Lonely Crusade. New York: Knopf, 1947.

Pinktoes. New York: G. P. Putnam's, 1965. Published in Paris by Olympia Press,

1961. In French, *Mamie Mason, ou un exercice de la bonne volonté*. Translated by Henri Collard. Paris: Plon, 1962.

Plan B. Paris: Lieu Commun, 1983.

The Primitive. New York: New American Library, 1955.

The Real Cool Killers. New York: Avon, 1959; reprint ed., Chatham, N.J.: Chatham Bookseller, 1973. In French, *Il pleut des coups durs*. Translated by Chantel Wourgraft. Paris: Gallimard, 1958. Titled originally "If Trouble Was Money."

Run Man Run. New York: G. P. Putnam's, 1966. In French, *Dare-dare*. Translated by Pierre Verrier. Gallimard, 1959.

The Third Generation. New York: World Publishing, 1954; reprint ed., Chatham, N.J.: Chatham Bookseller, 1973.

Autobiography

My Life of Absurdity. Garden City, N.Y.: Doubleday, 1976.

The Quality of Hurt. Garden City, N.Y.: Doubleday, 1972.

Collections

Black on Black: "Baby Sister" and Other Writings. Garden City, N.Y.: Doubleday, 1973. This anthology contains *Baby Sister* (screenplay, 1961); and the stories "A Nigger" (1937), "The Night's for Cryin'" (1937), "Headwaiter" (1938), "Pork Chop Paradise" (1938), "Lunching at the Ritzmore" (1942), "In the Night" (1942), "Heaven Has Changed" (1943), "Cotton Gonna Kill Me Yet" (1944), "All God's Chillun Got Pride" (1944), "Christmas Gift" (1944), "All He Needs Is Feet" (1945), "One More Way to Die" (1944), "Black Laughter" (1946), "Da-Da-Dee" (1948), "Mama's Missionary Money" (1949), "Tang" (1967), and "Prediction" (1969); and the articles "Now Is the Time! Here Is the Place!" (1942), "Zoot Riots Are Race Riots" (1943), "If You're Scared, Go Home!" (1944), and "Negro Martyrs Are Needed" (1944).

Short Stories Published Individually

"All God's Children Got Pride." *Crisis* 51 (June 1944):188–189, 204; also in Himes, *Black on Black*.

"All He Needs Is Feet." *Crisis* 50 (November 1943):332; also in Himes, *Black on Black*.

"Crazy in the Sir." *Esquire* 2 (August 1934):28, 114–16.

"Every Opportunity." *Esquire* 7 (May 1937):99, 129–30.

"Face in the Moon." *Coronet* 9 (February 1941):59–63.

"He Knew." *Abbott's Weekly and Illustrated News* (December 1933):15.

"He Seen It in the Stars." *Negro Story* 1 (July–August 1944):5–9.

"Heaven Has Changed." *Crisis* 50 (March 1943):78, 83; also in Himes, *Black on Black*.

"Her Whole Existence." *Abbott's Monthly* 6 (July 1933):25, 54.

"His Last Day." *Abbott's Monthly* 5 (November 1932):33, 61–63.
"I Don't Want to Die." *Abbott's Monthly* 6 (October 1933): 20–21.
"In the Night." *Opportunity* 20 (November 1942):334–35, 348–49; also in Himes, *Black on Black.*
"Let Me at the Enemy—An' George Brown." *Negro Story* 1 (December–January 1944–1945):9–18.
"Lunching at the Ritzmore." *Crisis* 49 (October 1942):314–15, 331; also in Himes, *Black on Black.*
"Make with the Shape." *Negro Story* 2 (August–September 1945):3–6.
"Mama's Missionary Money." *Crisis* 56 (November 1949):303; also in Himes, *Black on Black.*
"Marijuana and a Pistol." *Esquire* 13 (March 1940):58; also in Himes, *Black on Black.*
"Money Don't Spend in the Stir." *Esquire* 14 (April 1944):75.
"A Night of New Roses." *Negro Story* 2 (December–January 1945):10–14.
"The Night's for Cryin.'" *Esquire* 7 (January 1937):64, 146–48; also in Himes, *Black on Black.*
"One More Way to Die." *Negro Story* 2 (April–May 1946):10–14; also in Himes, *Black on Black.*
"A Penny for Your Thoughts." *Negro Story* 1 (March–April 1945):14–17.
"Salute to the Passing." *Opportunity* 17 (March 1939):74–79.
"The Snake." *Esquire* 52 (October 1943):302, 314–16.
"The Something in a Colored Man." *Esquire* 25 (January 1946):120, 158.
"The Song Says 'Keep on Smiling.'" *Crisis* 52 (April 1945):103–4.
"Strictly Business." *Esquire* 17 (February 1942):55, 128.
"There Ain't No Justice." *Esquire* 23 (April 1945):53.
"The Things You Do." *Opportunity* 19 (May 1941):141–43.
"To End All Stories." *Crisis* 55 (July 1946):205, 220.
"To What Red Hell." *Esquire* 2 (October 1934):100–101, 122, 127.
"Two Soldiers." *Crisis* 50 (January 1943):13, 29.
"The Visiting Hour." *Esquire* 6 (September 1936):76, 143–46.

Articles, Essays, and Reviews

"Democracy Is for the Unafraid." In Bucklin Moon, ed., *Primer for White Folks*, p. 81. New York: Doubleday, 1945.
"The Dilemma of the Negro Novelist in the United States." In John A. Williams, ed., *Beyond the Angry Black*, 52–58. New York: Cooper Square Publishers, 1966.
"Equality for 125,000 Dead." *Chicago Defender* (1945).
"Harlem ou le cancer de l'Amerique." *Présence africaine* 45 (Spring 1963):46–81.
"A Letter of Protest to His Publishers from Chester Himes in Spain." *Negro Digest* 18 (May 1969):98.
"Letter to New Masses about *Native Son*." *New Masses*, 21 May 1940, 23–24.

"Negro Martyrs Are Needed." *Crisis* 51 (May 1944):174.
"Now Is the Time! Here Is the Place!" *Opportunity* 20 (September 1942):272–73, 284.
"Reading Your Own." *New York Times Book Review,* 4 June 1967, 7.
"Review of *The Street* by Ann Petry." *New Masses* (1946).
"Zoot Suit Riots Are Race Riots." *Crisis* 50 (July 1943):20.
    Himes also contributed a series of unsigned articles "This Cleveland" to the *Cleveland Daily News* in 1939.

SECONDARY WORKS

Books

Kom, Ambroise. *Le Harlem de Chester Himes.* Quebec, Canada: Editions Naaman, 1978. A comprehensive study in French of Himes's relationship to both American and European literary traditions. Identifies Himes's "vast comedy" as a notable strength. Useful treatment of the French editions of Himes's novels and of the problems of translation.
Lundquist, James. *Chester Himes.* New York: Frederick Ungar Publishing Co., 1976. Survey of Himes's life and career, providing detailed summaries of early novels and perceptive treatment of the detective fiction.
Milliken, Stephen F. *Chester Himes, A Critical Appraisal.* Columbia: University of Missouri Press, 1976. Balanced and well-researched appraisal of Himes's career. "Racism, the hurts it inflicts, and all the tangled hates, is the dominant subject of the literary works" of Chester Himes.

Articles, Chapters of Books, and Reviews

Baldwin, James. "History as Nightmare." *New Leader* 30 (October 1947): 11, 15. Although finding formal and stylistic deficiencies in *Lonely Crusade*, Baldwin in an early review acknowledges Himes's artistic power. Compares novel to *Native Son*.
Berry, Jay R., Jr. "Chester Himes and the Hard-boiled Tradition." *Armchair Detective* 15 (1982):38–43. Traces the sources of Himes's detective fiction to Hammett and Chandler.
"Chester Himes et la Saga de Harlem." *Le Monde de livres* 13 (November 1970): 20–21. Includes an article by Michel Fabre and a brief interview.
Fabre, Michel. "*A Case of Rape*." *Black World* 21 (March 1972):39–48. Incisive assessment of this novel and the impact of French racism on Himes's literary vision.
————. "Chester Himes on la violence de L'étranger." In *La Rive noire: De Harlem à*

la Seine, 234–73. Paris: Lieu Commun, 1985. Establishes Himes as a major figure within the tradition of black expatriation in Paris.

Franklin, H. Bruce. "Two Novelists of the American Prison." In *The Victim as Criminal and Artist: Literature from the American Prison*, 181–237. New York: Oxford University Press, 1978. On Malcolm Braly and Himes. Perhaps the finest treatment of Himes's unique place in the American literary canon. "The novels of Chester Himes . . . provide a kind of miniature social history of the United States from World War II, through the days of the Black urban rebellions of the 1960's."

Gayle, Addison, Jr. *The Way of the New World*. Garden City, N.Y.: Doubleday, 1975. Perceptive treatment of *If He Hollers Let Him Go* and *Lonely Crusade* as studies in the "powerlessness" of the black middle-class intellectual. "It is as much to Chester Himes as Richard Wright that the young black writers of the present are indebted."

Hairston, Loyle. "Chester Himes—'Alien' in Exile." *Freedomways*, 7 November 1977, 14–18. Focuses on *My Life of Absurdity*. Takes a harsh, unsentimental view of Himes's failings and of an exile that "seems to have set him adrift in spiritual isolation."

Hard Boiled Dicks, nos. 8–9 (December 1983):1–95. Special Himes issue of this French publication. Articles by Michel Fabre, Yves Malartic, James Sallis, Claude LeRoy, and others. Bibliography.

Hernton, Calvin. Postscript to *A Case of Rape*. Washington, D.C.: Howard University Press, 1984. Thorough analysis of the last novel by Himes to be published in English. In *A Case of Rape*, Himes "explores the racism and sexism of interracial love and shows that when they occur together, the two factors mask each other and are virtually inseparable."

Lee, A. Robert. "Hurts, Absurdities and Violence: The Contrary Dimensions of Chester Himes." *Journal of American Studies* 12 (April 1978):99–114. A probing evaluation of the "existential contraries brought on by racism" that animate Himes's fiction. Excellent notes on publication history of Himes's texts.

————. "Making New: Styles of Innovation in the Contemporary Black American Novel." In Lee, ed., *Black Fiction: New Studies in the Afro-American Novel since 1975*, 222–50. New York: Barnes and Noble, 1980. Trenchant analysis of the experimental uniqueness of Himes's detective fiction. Terms him "a serious experimentalist and . . . one of America's senior literary native sons."

Margolies, Edward. "Chester Himes's Black Comedy: The Genre Is the Message." In *Which Way Did He Go: The Private Eye in Dashiell Hammett, Raymond Chandler, Chester Himes, and Ross MacDonald*, 53–70. New York: Holmes and Meier, 1982. A reliable and impressive overview of Himes's career. Treats Himes's "creation of grotesques" as the key to the art of his detective fiction.

————. "Race and Sex: The Novels of Chester Himes." In *Native Sons: A Critical Study of Twentieth Century Black American Authors*, 87–101. Philadelphia: J. B. Lippincott, 1968. A shrewd and balanced treatment of Himes as an

author who "regards the American scene as beyond redemption." Himes focuses on male-female relationships and has "an unabashed eye for the physical
and sensual."

———. "The Thrillers of Chester Himes." *Studies in Black Literature* (June
1970): 1–11. Himes sees Harlem as "the logical absurdity of the comic horror
of the black experience in America."

Micha, Rene. "Les Paroissiens de Chester Himes." *Les Temps modernes* (February
1965):567–84. On the fantastic world of Himes's detective fiction.

Nelson, Raymond. "Domestic Harlem: The Detective Fiction of Chester Himes."
Virginia Quarterly Review 48 (Spring 1972):260–76. Evaluates the
"newness" of Himes's detective fiction, especially its "grotesque comedy of violence." Traces Himes's increasingly experimental style, ending in *Blind Man
with a Pistol*, a "self-parody" of the genre.

Pfael, Fred. "Policiers noirs." *Nation*, 15 November 1986, 523–25. Comprehensive, well-written review of Himes's detective fiction and favorable overview of
his career. "The violent opening of each novel constitutes less a crime to be
solved than an overture promising more mayhem to come."

Reckley, Ralph. "The Oedipal Complex and Interracial Conflict in Chester Himes'
The Third Generation." *College Language Association Journal* 21 (December
1977):275–81. "The interracial conflict within the novel has its matrix in the
Oedipal Complex." A Freudian interpretation of the "incestuous love" that
Lillian Taylor lavishes on her son Charles.

———. "The Use of the Doppelgänger or Double in Himes's *Lonely Crusade*." *College Language Association Journal* 20 (June 1977):448–58. Treats Lester
McKinley and Luther McGregor as doubles to Lee Gordon. Sees in the names
Lee, Lester, and *Luther* a linguistic doubling of opposing selves, intensifying the
impact of racism on the black mate.

Reed, Ishmael. "Chester Himes: Writer." *Black World* (March 1972):23–38, 83–
86. A tribute to Himes, focusing on *The Quality of Hurt* and *Lonely Crusade*.
Alludes to the influence of Himes on John Williams, Ellison, Charles Wright,
Al Young, Clarence Major, and Reed himself. "He taught me the essential dif-
ferences between a black detective and Sherlock Holmes."

Rosenblatt, Roger. *Black Fiction*. Cambridge: Harvard University Press, 1974.
Evaluation of Bob Jones and his attempt in *If He Hollers Let Him Go* to avoid
"anonymity." Connects this theme to similar motifs in Wright and Ellison.

Sallis, James. "In America's Black Heartland: The Achievement of Chester
Himes." *Western Humanities Review* 37 (Autumn 1983):191–206. Con-
tends that the "naturalistic-didactic" and "apocalyptic" traditions define
Chester Himes's work.

Schraufnagel, Noel. *From Apology to Protest: The Black American Novel*.
Deland, Fla.: Everett Edwards, 1973. Surveys Himes's career from *If He
Hollers Let Him Go* to *The Primitive*, finding elements of both "protest"
and "assimilationism."

Smith, Robert P., Jr. "Chester Himes in France and the Legacy of the Roman Policier." *CLA Journal* 25 (September 1981):18–27. A general introduction to Himes's place within this tradition, with a deeper analysis of the French translation of *Cast the First Stone* (*Qu'on lu jette la première pierre*).

Williams, John A. "Chester Himes—My Man Himes." In *Flashbacks*, 292–97. Garden City, N.Y.: Doubleday, 1974, 292–97. Williams's preface to his extensive interview with the author is a graceful evocation of Himes as "perhaps the greatest naturalistic writer living today."

Yarborough, Richard. "The Quest for the American Dream in Three Afro-American Novels." *Melus* 8, no. 4 (1981):33–59. Evaluates *If He Hollers Let Him Go, The Street*, and *Invisible Man*.

Interviews

Fuller, Hoyt W. "Traveller on the Long, Rough, Lonely Old Road: An Interview with Chester Himes." *Black World* 21 (March 1972):4–22, 87–98.

Williams, John A. "Chester Himes—My Man Himes." In *Flashbacks: A Twenty-year Diary of Article Writing*, 292–352. Garden City, N.Y.: Doubleday, 1974.

Index